The Language of Qoheleth:
An Evaluation of the Recent Scholarly Studies

The Language of Qoheleth:
An Evaluation of the Recent Scholarly Studies

GNANARAJ D.

2012

The Language of Qoheleth: An Evaluation of the Recent Scholarly Studies — published by the Rev. Dr. Ashish Amos of the Indian Society for Promoting Christian Knowledge (ISPCK), Post Box 1585, Kashmere Gate, Delhi-110006.

© Author, 2012

All rights reserved. No part of this book may be reproduced or transmitted in any form or by any means, electronic, mechanical, photocopying, recording, or by any information storage and retrieval system, without the prior permission in writing from the publisher.

The views expressed in the book are those of the author and the publisher takes no responsibility for any of the statements.

ISBN: 978-81-8465-211-6

Laser typeset by
ISPCK, Post Box 1585, 1654, Madarsa Road, Kashmere Gate, Delhi-110006 • *Tel:* 23866323
e-mail: ashish@ispck.org.in • ella@ispck.org.in
website: www.ispck.org.in

To my parents
C. DEVARAJ and **ROSE THANGAM**
for their sacrifices, prayer,
inspiration and love

Contents

Dedication .... *v*
Acknowledgements .... *xi*
Abstract .... *xv*
Foreword .... *xvii*
Abbreviations .... *xix*
Introduction .... **xxiii**

CHAPTER 1
Early Observations on the Language of Qoheleth   1-21

The Language of Qoheleth until Twentieth Century	1
Earlier Studies until Delitzsch	2
Evaluation	5
The Contribution of Franz Delitzsch	5
The Impact of Delitzsch	7
Other Studies on the Language of Qoheleth	8
Twentieth Century: A Century of Debate	9
The First Phase: Theories and Responses	9
The Relative Consensus	18
The Second Phase: The Resurgence of the Debate	18

Current Research Trends	19
Summary of the Chapter	20

Chapter 2
Recent Studies on the Language of Qoheleth — 22-87

Bo Isaksson, Studies in the Language of Qoheleth, 1987	22
Methodology	23
Summary and Analysis	25
Conclusions of Isaksson	33
Evaluation of Isaksson	34
Daniel C. Fredericks, Qoheleth's Language: Re-Evaluating Its Nature and Date, 1988	36
Methodology	37
Summary and Analysis	38
Conclusions of Fredericks	48
Evaluation of Fredericks	49
Antoon Schoors, The Preacher Sought to Find Pleasing Words, Vol. 1, 2 (1991 / 2004)	52
Methodology	52
Summary and Analysis	53
Conclusions of Schoors	62
Evaluation of Schoors	64
Ian Young, Diversity in Pre-Exilic Hebrew, 1993	69
Methodology	71
Summary and Analysis	71
Conclusions of Young	76
Evaluation of Young	76

C. L. Seow, Linguistic Evidence to the Dating of Qoheleth, 1996	79
Methodology	79
Summary and Analysis	79
Conclusions of Seow	83
Evaluation of Seow	84
Summary of the Chapter	86

Chapter 3
The Language of Qoheleth:
Methodological Assessments and Proposals   88-128

General Concerns on the Recent Trend	89
The Three Scholarly Positions	89
The Pre-Exilic Period View	90
The Persian Period View	92
The Hellenistic Period View	93
The Perceived Stalemate	94
Will the Riddle of the Sphinx Ever Be Resolved?	96
Methodological *Impasse*	98
Inadequacies of Current Methodologies	98
Structural Linguistics	99
Lexical-Grammatical Analysis	100
Comparative Philology	100
The Diglossia Model	102
Observations on the Hurvitz-Polzin Paradigm	103

  The Methodological Rationale of Hurvitz   104
  Major Conclusions of Hurvitz-Polzin   106
  An Evaluation of Hurvitz-Polzin Paradigm   108
The Language of Qoheleth as Heterogeneous   112
  Archaic and Late Features in Qoheleth   113
    Archaic Features   113
    'Late' Features   116
    Observations and Evaluation   117
  Approaching the Problem of Qoheleth's Language   118
    Influence of Genre upon Qoheleth's Language   119
    Colloquialism in Qoheleth's Language   122
    A Case for a Non-Literary Hebrew   124
    Towards Formulating an Integrative Methodology   125
Summary of the Chapter   127

CONCLUSION **129-133**

BIBLIOGRAPHY **134-143**

Acknowledgements

A timely-help rendered in hour of need
Though small is greater than the world. *Thirukural*, 102.

As I pause to thank all who assisted me during the writing of this thesis, my heart overwhelms with gratitude. I honestly admit that I would not have completed this academic pursuit without such precious encouragements along the way.

I dare not hide my admiration towards my dear mentor Dr. Cristian G. Rata. Truly, I consider myself fortunate to have found in him an inspiring mentor, worthy of emulation (Pirke Avot 1:6). My earnest appreciation goes to Dr. Yoon Hee Kim for her prompt insights and illuminating suggestions. Special thanks also Dr. Tereso C. Casino, for his insights in further refining this thesis.

I am greatly indebted to Torch Trinity administration: President Rev. Dr. Young Jo Ha, Chair Person Dr. Hayng-Ja Lee for their vision, prayer and facilitating scholarship for my studies here. I also want thank the wonderful faculty, especially for the privilege of being able to *sit at the feet of* Dr. Kurtes Quesinberry, Dr. Steven Chang, Dr. Chul-Hae Kim and Dr. Julius Kim (Westminster Theological Seminary). I also extend my heartfelt thanks to Dr. Soon Jin Choi for his generous friendship, constant encouragements, genuine concern and prayers. Also, special thanks to Jeannie, Tina, Esther, Andy, Irene, Kyong Ha, Rev. Hong, Mrs. Kang, and other staff members for all of their kind assistance!

I have to thank Torch Trinity Library staff members for providing a very conducive environment for writing. In addition, Korean Bible Society Library, Seoul has been a valuable source for tracking down articles and various scholarly publications.

Also, my deep appreciation goes to Pr. Joshua Cho Jung Ho, for his prayers and encouragement. Pr. Jackson, for being a brilliant and understanding comrade; Pr. John David Samuel, for being a thoughtful and fantastic roommate for the last two years; Pr. Boipu Serto, for being a mature and constant friend. I do thank my beloved friends for their prayers and encouragements: Sanath Kumara, Joel Closa, Paul Teng, Maggie, and friends from various classes, small groups, vision groups, especially our amazing student council team 2008.

I thank Prof. Kim Chi Won, President of IAK for the opportunity to serve in IAK and accommodating my ever-changing work timing. I appreciate the IAK staff for their understanding. I want to extend a special thanks to Rev. Yoo Seung Dong, Senior Pastor of Inhudong Evangelical Holiness church (Jeonju) and all the members for their support and prayers. I also remember the fellow ministers and believers of Hansung Presbyterian Church English Ministry (Seoul) with gratitude. I also thank Pr. Paul Kim, Director of Ansan OMC, for being generous to accept my absences with grace and understanding and also for unwavering concern throughout our studies.

I also look back and thank my mentors: Rev. Dr. K. P. Yohannan for his passion for the Lost, Rev. Dr. Rajendren for his boldness in preaching the Word, Rev. Gnanadurai (Late) for being a spiritual father to me, and Mr. Raja Manickam (Late) for his dedication and role model as a teacher. Thanks to my dear brothers in ministry: Rev. V. T. Prince, Rev. Libini Singh, Rev. Jeba Singh, Rev. Sunil Francis, Abraham Isaac, and Bipin. They are always a joy to remember!

I acknowledge "that the book in its original form is the thesis submitted to Torch Trinity Graduate School of Theology towards the degree of Masters of Theology. The author is responsible for the title, contents and opinion expressed in it."

I give all the glory to my dear Lord for enabling me to complete this challenging task successfully. Truly He carried me on 'His eagle's wings.' *Soli Deo Gloria!*

Abstract

There is very little disagreement among scholars concerning the fact that Qoheleth employs a language quiet different from that of other books found in the wisdom corpus. A general reading of the book would bring to our attention linguistic usages, grammatical peculiarities and syntactical features that are unprecedented in other biblical books. While this tendency is noted by many scholars, the reasons proposed by them differ significantly from each other. This research attempts to investigate the position of the language of Qoheleth in the perspective of the current scholarship.

The analysis of the major studies led to the identification of three current scholarly positions: early date (Fredericks, Young and Isaksson), middle/Persian period view (Seow) and late/Hellenistic period view (Schoors). A stalemate in the current studies is perceived. And this stagnation is attributed to the methodological *impasse*. While the chronological model, developed and advocated by Hurvitz-Polzin, is found wanting as applied to the study of Qoheleth's language, the importance of approaching the language of Qoheleth from the linguistic diversity perspective was introduced after the works of Fredericks and Young. The explanations of genre and colloquialism have given some horizons for further exploration. And the case for non-literary Hebrew in Qoheleth, as an intentional part of Qoheleth's message should be given more attention. The challenge for future studies is incorporating the elements of chronological model along with the non-chronological model. This study also observes that the research horizons towards the language of Qoheleth have not been exhausted.

Foreword

The language of Qoheleth and its dating is still a vexing problem in the field of Old Testament scholarship, even if a definite majority of scholars tend to date the book late (this includes now many evangelical scholars).

The reality is, as demonstrated by Gnanaraj, that there has not been a systematic grammatical study of the language of Qoheleth that has been able to *prove* that its language is late. In this study, the author does an excellent job of reviewing the latest work on the language of Qoheleth (Isaksson, Fredericks, Schoors, Young, Seow etc.), their methodologies and shortcomings.

I highly recommend this work to anyone who is interested to learn more about Qoheleth, the history of the Hebrew language, and the latest works and methodologies employed to analyze the language of a biblical book.

Gnanaraj points out very well that there are no real parallels from the biblical times to the genre of Qoheleth, and "explanations of genre and colloquialism have given reasonable hope for the future research." Any scholar has to accept that, in a very real way, we are "working with no data," and it is very possible that we are dealing with non-literary Hebrew in Qoheleth.

Also, at the current stage of research in the book of Qoheleth, the "Aramaisms" argument rightly applied is not effective anymore for a late dating of the book. It would be more promising (and some studies are already underway) to study in depth the verbal system and other grammatical features of the book of Qoheleth (not only the lexicon). A well done comparison with the Hebrew text of Ben Sira should also help with the dating of Qoheleth.

It is with delight and satisfaction that I recommend this book on the study of the language of Qoheleth. It comes from a student who has struggled long and hard through laborious research to come to a clear understanding of this topic, one that is very difficult and still disputed. Gnanaraj, however, has succeeded wonderfully in clarifying the issues at stake, and in presenting the major works that deal with the language of Qoheleth.

His book is well worth reading and his suggestions for further studies are well worth pursuing.

The words of the wise are like goads, and like nails firmly fixed are the collected sayings; they are given by one Shepherd. Ecclesiastes 12:11

– Cristian G. Rață, Ph.D
Assistant Professor of Old Testament,
Torch Trinity Graduate University,
Seoul, South Korea,
July 06, 2011

Abbreviations

Books and Journals

ACCSOT	Ancient Christian Commentary on Scripture Old Testament
BBR	Bulletin for Biblical Research
BCOT	Baker Commentary on the Old Testament
BHQ	Biblia Hebraica Quinta
BHS	Biblia Hebraica Stuttgartensia
Bib	Biblica
BiTrans	The Bible Translator
BO	Bibliotheca Orientalis
CBQ	Catholic Biblical Quarterly
CTQ	Concordia Theological Quarterly
EJ	Encyclopedia Judaica
HA	Hebrew Abstracts
HAR	Hebrew Annual Review
HS	Hebrew Studies
HTR	Harvard Theological Review
HUCA	Hebrew Union College Annual
ICC	International Critical Commentary

IEJ	Israel Exploration Journal
Int	Interpretation
JANESCU	Journal of the Ancient Near Eastern Society of Columbia University
JAOS	Journal of American Oriental Society
JBL	Journal of Biblical Literature
JENS	Journal of Near Eastern Studies
JETS	Journal of Evangelical Theological Society
JHS	Journal of Hebrew Scripture
JJS	Journal of Jewish Studies
JNSL	Journal of Northwest Semitic Languages
JOTT	Journal of Translation and Text-linguistics
JP	Journal of Philology
JQR	Jewish Quarterly Review
JSJ	Journal for the Study of Judaism
JSOT	Journal for the Study of the Old Testament
JSOTSup	Journal for the Study of the Old Testament Supplement
JSS	Journal of Semitic Studies
JTS	Journal of Theological Studies
OTA	Old Testament Abstracts
OTE	Old Testament Essays
RBL	Review of Biblical Literature
S&I	Scripture and Interpretation
SJOT	Scandinavian Journal of Old Testament
SBLSP	Society of Biblical Literature Seminar Papers
TB	Tyndale Bulletin
Theo.	Themelios

UF	Ugarit Forschungen
VT	Vetus Testamentum
VTSup	Supplements to Vetus Testamentum
ZAW	Zeitschrift für die Alttestamentliche Wissenschaft

Technical Terms

4QQoh	Fragments of the Qoh Scrolls from Qumran
ABH	Archaic Biblical Hebrew
BA	Biblical Aramaic
BH	Biblical Hebrew
CH	Classical Hebrew
DSS	Dead Sea Scrolls
EBH	Early Biblical Hebrew
LBH	Late Biblical Hebrew
LXX	The Septuagint
MH	Mishnaic Hebrew
MT	Masoretic Text
QH	Qumran Hebrew
Qoh	Book of Qoheleth
SBH	Standard Biblical Hebrew
STH	Second Temple Hebrew

Introduction

The Significance of the Study

The Book of Qoheleth[1] commonly known as Book of Ecclesiastes, remains as an intricate puzzle in the Biblical canon.[2] The questions this book poses are very provocative, yet pragmatic; very unorthodox, yet realistic; very disturbing,

---

[1] Heb. "קֹהֶלֶת", qōhelet, feminine Qal participle, refers to the speaker in the book as well as the Hebrew title of the book. qōhelet comes from the root qhl, "to assemble or gather." James L. Cranshaw, *Ecclesiastes: A Commentary*, (Philadelphia: The West Minister Press, 1987), 56. Greek translation *ekklesiastes*, from which the English title emerges, refers to a speaker in an *ekklesiâ* (a local assembly). Iain Provan, *Ecclesiastes and Song of Songs, NIVAC* (Michigan: Zondervan, 2001), 28. After the silence in the early church until third CE, Qoheleth began to get more attention in the Christian tradition.

[2] Plumptree says, "It (Qoheleth) comes before us as the Sphinx of Hebrew Literature, with its unsolved riddles of history and life." Quoted by Addison G. Wright, "The Riddle of the Sphinx: The Structure of the Book of Qoheleth," *CBQ* 30 (1968), 313. Crenshaw says, "Qoheleth's radical views render his teachings an alien body within the Hebrew Bible", Crenshaw, *Ecclesiastes*, 22 and 52. Qoheleth has been viewed as "bizarre and something of a misfit within the biblical canon." Shannon Burkes, *Death in Qoheleth and Egyptian Biographies of the Late Period* (Atlanta: SBL, 1999), 1-8. There were disputes among early rabbinic schools of Shammai and Hillel regarding its canonical status (Mishnah Yadaim 3:5; Mishnah 'Eduyyot 5:3). Scott, *Proverbs and Ecclesiastes*, (New York: Doubleday, 1985), 191-192.

yet sensible. Many have attempted to approach Qoheleth from a theological perspective and made considerably varied observations due to the complexity of its theme.[3] Equal to the complexity of the theme of its discussion is the complexity of the language. There is no disagreement among scholars concerning the fact that Qoheleth employs a language quite different from that of other books found in the wisdom corpus.[4] A general reading of the book will draw the reader's attention to its unique linguistic usages, grammatical peculiarities and syntactical features that are unprecedented in other biblical books.[5] While this tendency is noted by many scholars, the reasons proposed by them differ significantly from each other.

The authorship of Qoheleth has been traditionally associated with King Solomon. Qoh 1:1 reads as follows, "The words of Qoheleth, son of David, King in Jerusalem."[6] The

---

[3] Christianson summarizes the current views as follows: "To Fox, he is a seeker of truth eager to communicate his experiences. To Frye, he is a realist embarked on a critique of the way of wisdom. To Paterson, he is a journal-keeping humanist. To Whybray, he is distinctly a Jewish Philosopher. To Zimmermann, he is a melancholy story teller." Eric S. Christianson, *A Time to Tell: Narrative Strategies in Ecclesiastes* (JSOTSup, 280; Sheffield: Sheffield Academic Press, 1998), 20-21.

[4] "Qoheleth's style of Hebrew, in both vocabulary and grammatical forms, is noticeably different from that in most of the rest of the Hebrew Bible," points Burkes. Shannon Burkes, *Death in Qoheleth*, 36-42. Rudman terms the language of Qoheleth as 'notoriously difficult.' Rudman: *Dating of Ecclesiastes*, 47.

[5] The language of the book of Job has also been at the heart of serious scholarly debates. See, the recent article. Cristian G. Rata, "Observations on the Language of the Book of Job", *S&I*, 1 (2008): 5-24.

[6] Gordis thinks that the Solomonic tradition guaranteed the book a place in the canon. See Robert Gordis, *Koheleth*, 42. But, Crenshaw argues that on the basis of its Torah-centric epilogue, it was accepted into the canon. See Crenshaw, *Ecclesiastes*, 52. However, it may be because of both that it was accepted in the canon.

period of its writing was assumed to be that of Solomon (10th BCE). However, since the 17th century scholars have entered into serious debate concerning the Hebrew used in Qoheleth.[7] Since then, Qoheleth has been understood as a book that was written in a language much closer to the language used in the *Mishnah*[8] thus belonging to a later period.[9]

In fact, linguistic evidence was used as the deciding factor to argue against the early period of composition: the near absence of *waw* imperfect consecutives, the increased use of *anî* to the exclusion of *anôchi*, frequent use of participles, the presence of two Persian words, the usage of *še*, the Aramaic coloring of the vocabularies and morphology, perceived Greek parallels, among others. These linguistic observations led to the general consensus that the language of Qoheleth does not represent an early period of composition. Also, this unique mixture of linguistic features guided few scholars to propose fancy theories which will be discussed later. While the theories were rejected in the subsequent years of study, it came to be

---

[7] See the very helpful summary of Schoors. Antoon Schoors, *The Preacher Sought to Find Pleasing Words I* (Leuven: Departement Orientalistiek, 1992), 1-6.

[8] Mishnah is one of the major literary works of Rabbinic Judaism. It contains the commentary on the written *Torah* by the group of rabbinic sages known as the Tannaim ("the repeaters") and redacted eventually about 200 CE by Rabbi Judah ha-Nasi. Brad H. Young, *Meet the Rabbis* (Peabody: Hendrickson, 2007), 82-83.

[9] Whitley dates this book very late (around 150 BCE). Charles F. Whitley, *Koheleth: His Language and Thought* (Berlin, New York: Walter de Gruyter, 1979), 137-139. Gordis dates it around 275 - 250 BCE, little earlier than Ben Sirach (190 - 180 BCE). Gordis, *Koheleth*, 62. Fox places it around 'fourth to third centuries BCE.' Michael Fox, *Qoheleth and His Contradictions*, (Sheffield: The Almond Press, 1989), 151. Seow places it around 450 BCE. C. L. Seow, "Linguistic Evidence and the Dating of Qoheleth", JBL 115/4 (1996), 665. Burkes agrees with Persian Period dating. See Burkes, *Death in Qoheleth*, 41.

held in general that Qoheleth resembles the language that is much closer to that of *Mishna* and the LBH books.

However, this debate which was arguably settled in the 1950s, resumed with vigor after the publication of the books by Isaksson[10] and Fredericks, who arrived at conclusions contrary to that of the consensus. Following this, Schoors have defended the consensus in his two volume study of the language of Qoheleth,[11] Seow took a slightly more conservative stand towards the Persian period date for Qoheleth.[12] Young has called the entire premise of holding Qoheleth as late book based on its language, invalid.[13]

The question is raised: What causes the studies on the language of Qoheleth to yield such varied conclusions? This research is an attempt to analyze the current studies on the language of Qoheleth and their methodologies in order to draw the trajectory for future language studies. Longman observes that "the language of the book is not a certain barometer of date."[14] However, it can be maintained that the study of the

---

[10] Bo Isaksson, *Studies in the Language of Qoheleth: With Special Emphasis on the Verbal System* (Uppsala: Acta Universitatis, 1987).

[11] Schoors has authored two books on the language of Qoheleth: Part I, published in 1992, deals with orthography, phonetics, morphology and syntax; whereas Part II, published in 2004, comprehensively deals with the vocabulary of Qoheleth.

[12] C. L. Seow, *Ecclesiastes: Anchor Bible* (London: Yale University Press, 1997).

[13] Ian Young, *Diversity in Pre-Exilic Hebrew* (Tubingen: Coronet Books Inc, 1993); Ian Young (ed.), *Biblical Hebrew: Studies in Chronology and Typology* (New York: T&T Clark International, 2003); Young, Ian, Robert Rezetko, and Martin Ehrensvärd, *Linguistic Dating of Biblical Texts*. 2 Vols. (London: Equinox, 2009).

[14] Tremper Longman, *The Book of Ecclesiastes* (Michigan: Eerdmans, 1998), 15. The emphasis of Longman's commentary is on the interpretation of the book and not on its language. So this generalized

language is the objective method currently available at our disposal to understand the period of writings which does not have the precise internal historical information required for dating. It is only when we understand the various factors that influenced and shaped the writer's language in the presentation of his unconventional philosophy that the grandeur of the *Sphinx of Hebrew Literature* would unfold before us into its fullest expression.

The Statement of the Research Problem

This research will attempt to investigate the following problem: Where should the language of Qoheleth be placed in the perspective of the current scholarship?

The Sub-Problems

The first sub-problem: How did the debate on the language of Qoheleth develop? The second sub-problem: What are the current scholarly approaches and proposals that interact with the language of Qoheleth? The third sub-problem: What are the methodological concerns for future investigations on the language of Qoheleth?

The Basic Assumptions

This research presupposes the following assumptions:

The first basic assumption is that the Hebrew language evolved throughout the centuries and the changes are possibly observable in the writings which come from various periods.

The second basic assumption is that the evaluation of the major scholarly studies, their approaches and proposals contribute to the discussion on the language of Qoheleth.

---

statement should be taken as a attitude of disappointment towards the contribution of language studies in general and toward the language of Qoheleth in particular.

The third basic assumption is that the language of Qoheleth belongs to a certain period in the history of the Hebrew language, though it is not the only criterion for its chronological placement.

Methodology

This research is based on a detailed evaluation of the recent approaches that specifically engages the language of Qoheleth. It employs the descriptive-textual analysis to study the language of Qoheleth. This research will be dependent on existing literary resources which include books, journal articles and other electronic sources.

The Definition of Terms

In this context, "Language" refers to the kind of Hebrew employed in the process of writing the book of Qoheleth.

Qoheleth refers to the book as a whole, rather than addressing to the writer of the book who also identifies himself as Qoheleth (1:1, 2, 12, 7:27, 12:9, 10).

The phrase "Recent Scholarly Studies" distinguishes the few books/articles that best represent the current debate. This includes the works of Isaksson, Fredericks, Schoors, Young, and Seow.

The resurgence of study on the language of Qoheleth took place after the publication of Isaksson's book. Though the sources written after this period will be consulted, the main focus will be on the works since Isaksson.

Delimitations

This study is limited to specifically understanding the language of Qoheleth. It is beyond the scope of this research to engage in discussions over its theology, other issues of contention such as authorship, internal literary unity, or issues that are not directly related to the study of the language. The entire book will be approached solely from the linguistic standpoint as best represented by the current scholarship.

1
Early Observations on the Language of Qoheleth

This chapter sets out to review the history of scholarship on the language of Qoheleth. It also presents an objective evaluation of the past scholarship that paved formidable foundations for the on-going debate on the language of Qoheleth. And, the appraisal of this chapter would funnel the trajectory of the research to the current trends, which will be further elaborated in the subsequent chapter.

THE LANGUAGE OF QOHELETH UNTIL TWENTIETH CENTURY

Since 17th century, occasional observations have been made on the language of Qoheleth. This section reviews such early observations. Some of those who acknowledged the atypical linguistic features in Qoheleth argued for an early date, others were convinced it was written in a late period.[1] The debate

---

[1] C. D. Ginsburg, *Coheleth, Commonly Called the Book of Ecclesiastes* (London: Ktav Publishers, 1861), 100ff.

was chiefly connected with the question of authorship and the linguistic data was used to counter the Solomonic authorship for Qoheleth. And the scholarly opinion was inconclusive.

Earlier Studies until Delitzsch

Early Christian commentators of Qoheleth generally assumed Solomonic authorship and dated it to 10th BCE. Ginsburg devotes around 150 pages to summarize the significant works on Qoheleth until 1860.[2] He observes the absence of early Christian references to Qoheleth until the first half of the third century.[3] Then allegorical interpretations prevailed in the early centuries, aligned with the conventional rabbinical views.[4] There was no challenge to the authorship of Solomon until 16th CE.[5] It was Luther (1532 CE) who made the observation: "Solomon himself has not written the book of Ecclesiastes, it was compiled by Sirach at the time of Maccabees."[6] However, his opinion did not become a mainstream view until a century later.

The seventeenth century shows a surge of interest in Qoheleth studies. Importantly, the earliest observation on the language of Qoheleth comes from the 17th century politician-

---

[2] Ginsburg's commentary was published in 1861. It remains valuable for its review of the early scholarship.

[3] Gregory Thaumaturgus wrote the first metaphrase of Ecclesiastes (270 CE). John Jarick, *Gregory Thaumaturgus's Paraphrase of Ecclesiastes* (Atlanta: Scholars Press, 1990), 3.

[4] Jerome is the father of allegorical interpretation in the Latin Church. The purpose of his commentary on Qoheleth was to steer Blesilla, a Roman young lady, towards monastic life. Ginsburg, *Coheleth*, 101.

[5] *Ibid.*, 109-112. However, Didymus the Blind (313-398 CE) allows the possibility of non-Solomonic authorship. J. Robert Wright, "Ecclesiastes," *ACCSOT IX* (Illinois: IVP, 2005), 192.

[6] *Ibid.*, 113. Luther, not in his commentary, but in his *Table Talk*, denies Solomonic authorship. Craig G. Bartholomew, "Ecclesiastes," *BCOT* (Grand Rapids: Baker Academic, 2009), 33.

lawyer-theologian Hugo de Groot (H. Grotius). He observed many words in Qoheleth which are only found in the exilic/post-exilic works such as Daniel, Ezra, etc.[7] And from then on, the argument against Solomonic authorship gradually gained ground.[8] It's important to note this here because this comment has left a lasting influence upon the course of future studies.[9] Though Grotius' statement is a general observation, his contribution is that he noticed the unusual and unconventional usage of language in comparison to exilic/post-exilic books. It had gradually led many exegetes to conclude that the book of Qoheleth was written at a much later date.[10]

In the following two centuries, there was remarkable advancement of scholarship in the line of Grotius' linguistic argument. Bishop Lowth's comment on Qoheleth is noteworthy from the 18th century. He held the opinion that the Solomonic authorship of Qoheleth was unlikely:

> "The language is generally low. I might almost call it mean or vulgar; it is frequently loose, unconnected, approaching to the incorrectness of conversation; and possess very little of the poetical character, even in the composition and structure of the periods."[11]

Some early notable scholars who affirmed the non-Solomonic authorship (by extension, a later date) for Qoheleth are as

---

[7] Bianchi quotes Grotius' statement: "Ego tamen Solomonis esse non puto, sed scriptum serius sub illius regist tamquam poenitentia ducti nomine. Argumentum eius rei habeo multa vocabula quae non alibi quam in Daniele, Esdra et Chalddaeis interpretibus reperias." Bianchi, "The Language of Qoheleth: A Bibliographical survey," ZAW 105 (1993), 211.

[8] After Luther, Grotius affirmed Qoheleth's non-Solomonic authorship. Ginsberg, *Coheleth*, 1ff.

[9] Bianchi: The Language of Qoheleth, 211.

[10] *Ibid.*, 1-2.

[11] Quoted by Schoors, *Pleasing Words I*, 1.

follows: J. C. Doderlin favored exilic period citing the lateness of the language (1784); G. Zirkel argued for Greek influence upon the grammar and syntax of Qoheleth (1792) and dated it in the Hellenistic age; H. G. A. Ewald pointed out its deviation from the Biblical Hebrew and the Aramaic color and places it in the end of Persian period (1837-1867); etc.[12] This period also witnessed the gradual abandonment of Solomonic authorship for Qoheleth.

However, the proponents of Solomonic authorship explained the linguistic peculiarities in varied ways. Bianchi notes two scholars who explained the linguistic features in favor of early date: E. Boehl noted that "the Aramaisms penetrated into Hebrew from the Solomonic age as did the Persian word *pitgam* (8:5) and *pardesim* (2:5)."[13] Vegni reasoned that Solomon might have known them through his trading partners or they were common in the cognates of Solomonic era.[14] Schoors gives a list of pro-Solomonic scholars of 18th and 19th century.[15] However, there was no systematic linguistic study done in favor of the early date.

Under such circumstances, Qoheleth was generally thought to be the production of later times, between the Persian era to first century CE.[16] And the defense for the Pro-Solomonic preference was waning during this period. What was lacking

---

[12] *Ibid.*, note 4, 2.

[13] Bianchi: The Language of Qohelet, 211.

[14] *Ibid.*, 211. Van der Palm noted that Solomon knew *'pardes'* from his Persian concubines. Schoors, *Pleasing Words I*, 3.

[15] Schoors, *Pleasing Words I*, note 8, 2.

[16] See the summary of Archer on the early scholarship of Qoheleth. G. L. Archer, "The Linguistic Evidence for the Date of Ecclesiastes," *JETS* 7/3 (1969), 167.

was a comprehensive study on the language to support the claims of date, be it early or late.[17]

Evaluation

The debate in the Pre-Delitzsch era was due to the identification of differences in the style, vocabularies (foreign words) and uncommon grammatical patterns found in Qoheleth. These observations were fragmentary and scattered. There was no comprehensive study, done on the language of Qoheleth. However, certain insights that were received from the discussion of this era continued to illuminate the scholarly world.

This period of time in the history of interpretation is important especially to understand the development of the linguistic argument, and not for its contribution on the language of Qoheleth itself. However, it paved the way for the expansion of the field of research in the following centuries.

The Contribution of Franz Delitzsch

Franz Delitzsch was a remarkable German theologian and an accomplished Hebraist.[18] His commentary on Koheleth was published in 1875.[19] He was the first scholar to analyze the language of Qoheleth in detail, and most importantly, "to sum up the grammatical and lexical evidences in favor of a late date

---

[17] *Ibid.*, 167-168.

[18] Delitzsch had authored a commentary series with Keil which is still in use. He wrote on diverse fields such as Jewish history, Christian apologetics, Biblical interpretation and etc. He is well known for his translation of Greek New Testament into Hebrew. Even today, his translation is considered as the standard version among the Hebrew Christian community. "F. Delitzsch," *www.en.wikipedia.org/wiki/Franz_Delitzsch* (Accessed Nov 28, 2008).

[19] Delitzsch, *Proverbs, Ecclesiastes, Song of Solomon*, trans., M. G. Easton (Grand Rapids: Eerdmans, 1975).

for Qoheleth which was scattered in the works of his predecessors."[20] His studies have had a vast significance in the following centuries until now.

Delitzsch's contribution towards the language of Qoheleth can be summarized briefly as follows: [21]

a. Qoheleth contains extensive late vocabulary that is found in the post-Biblical literatures. He lists 96 *hapax legomenon* and points that they were frequently used in the later centuries.

b. Grammatical traits that belong to the late phase of Hebrew, such as the interchange of ל"א and ל"ה forms.

c. The changing aspect of the verbs: The use of imperfect consecutive in unusual form (4:1, 7 and 1:17).

d. The Perfect is followed by *ʾānî*.

e. The widespread use of the participle, a phenomenon well attested in the post-exilic books.

f. The use of *zeh*: It has been used in diverse ways and forms in Qoh, the usage which points to the lateness.

Based on these observations, Delitzsch argued for the late date for Qoheleth and defended the non-Solomonic authorship.[22] He believed that the language employed by Qoheleth reflected a lot of transitional traits that were characteristics of the later Jewish Baraita literatures and Mishnaic period. To Delitzsch, the usage of the relative particle שׁ and the presence of Aramaisms, among others, seem to

---

[20] Schoors, *Pleasing Words I*, 2.

[21] Delitzsch, *Ecclesiastes*, 190-201.

[22] Delitzsch argued for a Persian period dating, but the later scholars claimed even much later date. *Ibid.*, 190. And also see, Seow: Linguistic Evidence, 643.

suggest a late composition.[23] Thus, he concluded that Qoheleth could not have been written earlier in the time of Solomon or in the pre-exilic period. He claimed that "the language of Qoheleth is connected, yet loosely with the old language, but at the same time it is in full accord with that New Hebrew we meet in the Mishna."[24] The following section shows how his contributions continued to influence the later scholarship well into the modern times.

The Impact of Delitzsch

Barton astutely remarks that "the linguistic argument for the non-Solomonic authorship has been worked out to a complete demonstration by the masterly hand of the late Franz Delitzsch."[25] Indeed, Delitzsch had left an indelible mark upon the future course of research. Every work after him either expanded or merely restated his conclusions. Also the following quote by Delitzsch, "If the book of Kohelth were of old Solomonic origin, then there is no history of the Hebrew language"[26] went on to become one of the most quoted comments in the post-Delitzsch era works on Qoheleth.[27] This strongly proves the lasting influence of Delitzsch upon Qoheleth studies.

Also the successive Qoheleth scholarship has been modeled to think in the framework that was set by him. Bianchi precisely observes that "Delitzsch's analysis shaped all the following

---

[23] From the list of his *hapax legomenon*, he had concluded that they mainly occurred in the Mishnaic literatures. Bianchi: The Language of Qoheleth, 212.

[24] Delitzsch, *Ecclesiastes*, 197.

[25] G. A. Barton, *Critical and Exegetical Commentary on the Book of Ecclesiastes, ICC* (Edinburgn: T&T Clark, 1906), 22.

[26] Delitzsch, *Ecclesiastes*, 190.

[27] Longman, *Ecclesiastes*, 4.

studies about Qoheleth's language."[28] And until now, the majority of Qoheleth scholarship has not broken free from the effects of his research and its haunting conclusions.[29]

Other Studies on the Language of Qoheleth

Siegfried contributed significantly to the language of Qoheleth.[30] Schoors observes that, "Siegfried is as exhaustive as Delitzsch and more systematic, for he divides the evidence into grammar, i.e., morphology and syntax and vocabulary, the latter subdivided into Rabbinism, Late Hebraisms, Aramaisms and Grecisms."[31] He dated Qoheleth into the Hellenistic period.

Bianchi mentions other scholars who followed the trails left by Delitzsch and furthered the research on the language of Qoheleth. "W. Nowack, C. Siegfried, G. Wildeboer, V. Zapletal and G. A. Barton closely quoted many of Delitzsch's linguistic arguments. They stated some peculiar problems, such as the emergence of the name endings *ût, ôn, îon*, the Aramaisms *zemân*, the Mishnaisms *hepæs* (5:3) or *taqqen* (7:13)."[32] Among those who opted for the later date for Qoheleth were disagreements of how late it should be dated: some favored the late Persian period while others suggested a date in the Hellenistic period. The rationale for dating into the Hellenistic era was due to the perceived historical allusions. However, Bianchi pointed out the problem that "no criterion is more

---

[28] Bianchi: The Language of Qohelet, 212.

[29] After a century later, Murphy begins the section on "Language, style and Form" with this famous quote from Delitzsch and affirms that, "there is general agreement that the language (of Qoheleth) is late." See, Murphy, Ecclesiastes, *WBC*, xxvii.

[30] Siegfried introduced source-critical approach to Qoh. C. Siegfried, *Prediger and Hoheslied* (Göttingen: Vandenhoeck and Ruprecht, 1898).

[31] Schoors, *Pleasing Words I*, 2.

[32] Bianchi: The Language of Qohelet, 212.

problematic in Qoheleth's research than the historical one since it is possible to find different historical allusions behind every verse."[33] It strongly negates the possibility of dating based on historical allusions.

Also, study on the language not only dealt with the question of dating. Scholars like Knobel approached the language of Qoheleth as a means to express philosophical thoughts, a view that was later expounded by Gordis and others.[34] At the turn of the 20th century, Renan, a French scholar, emphasized Mishnaisms (over Aramaisms) and dated Qoh around 1 BCE.[35] But the predominant scholarship maintained the mixture of Aramaisms and Mishnaisms in Qoheleth's language. And so, Renan's views did not garner enough support among the scholars.

TWENTIETH CENTURY: A CENTURY OF DEBATE

The debate on the language of Qoheleth began to accelerate at the turn of the 20th century. This century offers some of the intensifications of the earlier conclusions and the formulation of new theories that led to ardent debates in the subsequent decades. Their inevitable reflexes are still felt in the current research trends. And, it has been facilitated by the emergent knowledge of the cognates, a plethora of discoveries of numerous ancient texts and the application of modern linguistics upon the Biblical texts. However, the language of Qoheleth remained precisely indefinable and its date unsettled as ever.

The First Phase: Theories and Responses

Largely due to Delitzsch and his devoted successors, the position that the language of Qoheleth belongs to the later date

---

[33] *Ibid.*, 212.
[34] Schoors, *Pleasing Words I*, 3.
[35] Bianchi: The Language of Qohelet, 212.

began to gather momentum in the early twentieth century.[36] Barton summarized their views in his commentary as follows:

> "The Hebrew in which the book of Ecclesiastes is written exhibits some of the latest developments of the language which appear in the Old Testament. The decadent character of the tongue, as here employed, appeared in the use of Aramaic and Persian words, the employment of late words used elsewhere only in the Mishna; in the use of late developments and mixtures of Hebrew forms, the absence or infrequent use of characteristic constructions, such as *waw* consecutive, and the frequent employment of syntactical constructions rare in the older books."[37]

The high frequency of Aramaisms and the plausible influence of Aramaic upon the morphology and grammar were taken to suggest a late date.[38] Mroczek observes, "on this basis (and of the basis of the other linguistic features, such as "Mishnaisms"), Qoheleth was aligned with Ezra-Nehemiah, Chronicles and Esther..."[39] The objective of such deductions were mainly to show the similarities between the language of Qoheleth with that of LBH and MH, and to establish a later date, from the late Persian period to 1st BCE. However, this research acumen gradually began to lead toward a different unexpected curve.

As Bianchi observes, "... some scholars began to hypothesize about a different solution for Qoheleth's linguistic peculiarities: Qoheleth may have written this book not in Hebrew but in another language, whose influence could still

---

[36] Schoors, *Pleasing Words I*, note 10, 3.

[37] Barton, *Ecclesiastes*, 52.

[38] For example, the commentary of E. Podechard (1912) also stressed the importance of Aramaisms in the book. Later his views were accepted by scholars such as H. W. Hertzberg (1932) and K. Galling (1940). Bianchi: The Language of Qohelet, 213.

[39] Eva Mroczek, "Aramaisms in Qohelet: Methodological Problems in Identification and Interpretation," Issues in Hebrew Philology, Unpublished paper, (2008), 2.

be perceived in the translation."[40] Margoliouth pioneered such a view and inferred that there are many Phoenician loanwords which are explicable only if Qoheleth is taken as a translation. He took it as an Indo-Germanic work which was customized for the Jewish populace by a Jewish editor who sprayed the book with Jewish references such as God, David, etc.[41] Though this view was not accepted by the scholars who were preoccupied with the prevalence of Aramaisms and Mishnaisms, it was successful in casting a new perspective.

Few years later, Burkitt argued that "what we have is not an original, but a translation;... if it be a translation, it is naturally a translation of the Aramaic."[42] He reasoned that the laborious and un-Hebraic style of the language can't be natural to Hebrew formations. Fernandez critiqued this view by questioning the plausible audience and reiterated that the allusion to Solomon as the author assumes Hebrew as the original language of composition.[43] However, after two decades, this theory was expanded and advanced by three major Old Testament scholars: F. Zimmermann, C. C. Torrey and H. L. Ginsberg. Zimmermann defended and expanded the theory proposed by Burkitt.[44] Schoors sums up Zimmermann's position:

"...[Zimmermann] defended the theory on several grounds: viz. the presence of Aramaic words in the text, the inexact

---

[40] Bianchi: The Language of Qohelet, 213.

[41] D. S. Margoliouth, "Ecclesiastes," *Jewish Encyclopedia*, Vol 12 (1901-1907), 32-36.

[42] F. C. Burkitt, "Is Ecclesiastes a Translation?" *JHS* 22 (1921), 22-23.

[43] A. Fernandez, "Es El Ecclesiastés una Versión?" *Bib* 3 (1922): 45-50.

[44] F. Zimmermann, "The Aramaic Provenance of Qohelet," *JQR* 36 (1945-46): 17-45.

status of nouns in Qoh (i.e. the irregular use of the article);⁴⁵ the mistranslations (he presents some 25 examples, seven of which he considers as strong case); the confusion of הוא and [הוּא]; quid pro quo renderings; the confusion of the tense; grammatical and exegetical difficulties which are solved by the application of the translation theory."⁴⁶

He held that the author was a Babylonian Jew who knew Aramaic and Akkadian and served the court of Anthiocus III at Antiochia or Selucia in the last quarter of the third century BCE.⁴⁷ The original was composed in East-Aramaic, somewhat close to the language of Babylonian Talmud, in Syriac and partly in Targums. And the Hebrew translation was made somewhere in 190 BCE. ⁴⁸ He pointed out the influence of Aramaic upon Qoheleth's morphology and these views continue to exert influence in certain circles.

C. C. Torrey explained that the linguistic proximity between Aramaic and Hebrew makes it difficult to exactly pinpoint the translation from a language to the other. Though he did not entirely agree with Zimmermann, he asserted that Zimmermann

---

⁴⁵ Bianchi thinks that this theory was very influential as it was able to explain the volatile use of the definite article. Bianchi: The Language of Qohelet, 214. Zimmermann explained: "the article juts up peculiarly when it is clearly unnecessary, yet on the other hand, the article is lacking when it should be present. Even more cogently, the article appears and disappears mysteriously in nouns following one another in a series. This was due to the translator who failed to observe the distinction between the absolute and the Emphatic state in Aramaic." He thought that the translator by adding and omitting the articles in random way, added to the complexity of the text. F. Zimmermann, "The Question of Hebrew in Qoheleth," *JQR* 40 (1949-50) 98. Also, F. Zimmermann, *The Inner World of Qoheleth* (New York: Ktav Publishers, 1973), 128-131.

⁴⁶ Schoors, *Pleasing Words I*, 7.

⁴⁷ *Ibid.*, 7.

⁴⁸ F. Zimmermann: The Question of Hebrew in Qoheleth, 79ff.

was right in his fundamental assumptions.[49] He held that Qoheleth's language was distinctly Aramaic and it seems like the Aramaic idioms are literally rendered in Hebrew. He also quoted and expanded on the studies of Zimmermann. H. L. Ginsburg also supported and expanded on Zimmermann's views.[50]

Gordis vigorously opposed this view as soon as Zimmermann advocated it. He held that Qoheleth probably knew and spoke Aramaic but rejected the translation theory.[51] He argued,

> "It may be maintained that the difficult text may be presumed to be the original rather than a translation... and Zimmermann's arguments would only prove that Qoheleth was written in Hebrew, by a writer who, like all his contemporaries, knew Aramaic and probably used it freely in daily life."[52]

Gordis explained the grammatical peculiarities by assuming the employment of an unusual type of Hebrew which is different from classical Hebrew. He concluded that "the language of Qoheleth marks the transition between Biblical and Mishnaic Hebrew."[53] Bianchi observes, "Gordis arguments, and

---

[49] He feared that Zimmerman weakened his case by overdoing the demonstration. C.C. Torrey, "The Question of Original Language of Qoheleth," *JQR 39* (1948-49), 152.

[50] To him, the plural of *pardēsîm* betrayed Aramaic influence: the plural of *pardēs* in Aramaic is *pardēsîn*, but in post-Biblical Hebrew, it is *pardēsôt*. He emphasized the irregular of definite articles, mistranslations and the confusion between הוא and הוּא. H. L. Ginsburg, *Koheleth* (Tel Aviv: M. Newman, 1961).

[51] Robert Gordis, "The Original Language of Qoheleth," *JQR 38* (1946-47), 83.

[52] Gordis: The Original Language, 70. "The Translation Theory of Qoheleth Re-Examined," *JQR 40* (1949-50), 103-116.

[53] Gordis, *Koheleth*, 42.

the following discovery at Qumran of a Qoheleth's scroll[54] – dated by Muilenburg around 150 BCE – doomed the Aramaic translation hypothesis."[55] The critique of the translation theory is best articulated in the words of Schoors:

> "This is a self-destructive theory, for why should somebody want to translate an Aramaic text into Hebrew when he neither properly understands the Aramaic original nor sufficiently masters the Hebrew language to offer flawless translation. For a few mistranslations can betray the translational character of a text, but in the theory under consideration there are too many of them and they are too fundamental. It is also strange that a translation would have left so many downright Aramaisms (untranslated)."[56]

In spite of the reputations of the defending scholars, with the vigorous opposition of Gordis, the translation theory was abandoned. However, Qoheleth's unique style of Hebrew had to be explained. At this juncture, Dahood proposed a theory to illuminate the eccentric language of Qoheleth: Canaanite-Phoenician Theory.[57] Dahood followed D. S. Margoliouth, who

---

[54] Two manuscripts were found in Qumran: 4QQoh^a and 4QQoh^b. They were dated, on paleographic grounds, to the second quarter of the second century BCE. See, Seow: Linguistic Evidence, 643. The discoveries and the dating is explained with detail in the following articles: J. Muilenburg, "A Qoheleth Scroll from Qumran," *BASOR 135* (1954) 20-28. F. M. Cross, "The Oldest Manuscript from Qumran," *JBL 74* (1955), 153-162. E. Ulrich, "Ezra and Qoheleth Manuscripts from Qumran," in *Priests, Prophets and Scribes*, (Sheffield: JSOT Press, 1992), 139-157.

[55] Bianchi: The Language of Qohelet, 216.

[56] Schoors, *Preachers Vol 1*, 8.

[57] Mitchell Dahood, "Canaanite-Phoenician Influence in Qoheleth," *Biblia 33* (1952), 30-52; "The Language of Qoheleth" *CBQ 14* (1952), 227-232; "Qoheleth and Recent Discoveries," *Biblia 39* (1958), 302-318; Qoheleth and North West Semitic Philology," *Biblia 46* (1962), 349-365; "Canaanite Words in Qoheleth 10.20," *Biblia 46* (1965), 210-212; "The Phoenician Background of Qoheleth," *Biblia 47* (1966), 264-282; "Scriptio Defectiva in Qoheleth 4.10a," *Biblia 49* (1968), 243; "Three Parallel Pairs

earlier evoked Phoenician influence upon Qoheleth, in establishing his theory.⁵⁸ He was also encouraged by W. F. Albright who favored Canaanite influence in his personal research.⁵⁹ Dahood argued that "the author of the book was a Jew who wrote in Hebrew but who employed Phoenician spelling and whose language was heavily influenced by Phoenician vocabulary and style."⁶⁰ He strongly believed that "only when the Northern origin of this enigmatic book is recognized will the mystery which surrounds it be dispelled."⁶¹

Dahood held that the Phoenician influence upon Qoheleth entered in three ways: the orthography, the language and the history. With regard to Qoheleth's orthography, he argued that any work employing the Hebrew orthography of the fourth-third century BCE would've been amply supplied with *matres lectionis*.⁶² But, "many of the variants in the Hebrew manuscripts and in the versions can be accounted for by supposing that the original author did not use *matres lectionis*, a feature peculiar to Phoenician at the time of Qoheleth's composition in the late fourth or early third century BCE."⁶³ His grammatical remarks: the demonstrative pronoun *zeh* written defectively as *z* has to be related with Phoenician

---

in Ecclesiastes 10.18: A Reply to Prof. Gordis," *JQR* 62 (1971), 84-87; Northwest Semitic Philology and Three Biblical Texts," *JNSL* 2 (1972), 17-22. "The Independent Pronoun in the Oblique Case in Hebrew," *CBQ* 34 (1972), 87-90.

⁵⁸ Archer: The Linguistic Evidence, 171.

⁵⁹ Albright, Dahood's mentor, held that, "there is a veritable flood of allusions to Canaanite (Phoenician) literature in Hebrew works composed between the seventh and third BCE." W. F. Albright, *From Stone Age to Christianity*, 243.

⁶⁰ Dahood: The Language of Qoheleth, 227.

⁶¹ *Ibid.*, 232.

⁶² Dahood: Canaanite-Phoenician Influence, 36.

⁶³ Dahood: The Language of Qoheleth, 227.

morphology;⁶⁴ relative pronoun *šæ* is a Phoenician feature;⁶⁵ the irregular use of article is seen in Phoenician inscriptions.⁶⁶ Dahood allowed Aramaic and Mishnaic influence but they entered Hebrew through Phoenician. He found the prevalent use of commercial vocabularies in Qoheleth to be pointing to commerce-centered Phoenician culture.⁶⁷

However, Dahood's theory did not find mainstream support. Gordis argued against it.⁶⁸ And even if such Canaanite influence is found in Qoheleth, it has to be expected as Whitley observes: "indeed it would be unscientific exegesis ... if we were to deny him [Qoheleth] an acquaintance with the traditions of a remarkable Canaanite culture."⁶⁹ Fredericks further points out the major weakness of Dahood's theory: "Much of Dahood's vocabulary parallels with Phoenician and Ugaritic has BH precedent and are not any indication of Phoenician-Canaanite influence."⁷⁰ Also on the philosophical grounds, the theory was questioned. As Bianchi summarizes,

> "In his attempt to explain the Canaanite linguistic features in Qohelet, Dahood assumed the existence of a Phoenician wisdom tradition as well as the presence of the school of philosophy in Phoenicia during the fourth and third century

---

[64] *Ibid.*, 228.

[65] *Ibid.*, 228-229.

[66] *Ibid.*, 231.

[67] Schoors, *Pleasing Words I*, 9.

[68] Gordis argued, "[Dahood's] study has revealed some interesting parallels between Phoenician and Punic on the one hand, and Biblical Hebrew in general, on the other. This is a situation to be expected in view of the close kinship of both languages and literatures... on the other hand, we do not find evidence of specific influence from Phoenician on the orthography, morphology and syntax of Koheleth." Gordis, "Was Qoheleth a Phoenician? Some Observations on the Methods of Research" *JBL* 74 (1955): 103-114.

[69] Whitely, "Qoheleth and Ugaritic Parallels," *UF* 11 (1979), 824.

[70] Fredericks, *Qoheleth's Language*, 21.

BCE. However, neither a Phoenician wisdom tradition, nor the influence of Phoenician philosophers upon those of Greeks has so far been proved."[71]

Consequently, the mainstream scholarship flocked behind Gordis and rejected Dahood's theory. Interestingly, G. L. Archer argued that the theory of Dahood was not completely negated by Gordis. He observed:

> "All the alleged Aramaisms cited by Gordis were thoroughly discussed by Dahood and shown to point equally well towards a Phoenician provenance. If this, then, is the best rebuttal that can be brought against the theory of a Phoenician background for *Ecclesiastes*, it is only reasonable to conclude that it (Phoenician theory) stands confirmed and vindicated."[72]

But, Archer did not agree with the post-exilic date for Qoheleth. Rather he used the conclusions of Dahood to support the early dating of Qoheleth to 10 century BCE.[73] And this view of Archer also did not find support in the later studies.

However, Dahood has shown some of the very fascinating parallels between the Qoheleth and Canaanite literature. According to Seow, "most suggestive of all is the expression תַּחַת הַשָּׁמֶשׁ "under the sun" ... this expression is found twice in Phoenician, in the inscriptions of Kings Tabnit and Eshmunazor of Sidon (KAI 13:7-8; 14.12)."[74] Dahood remained as a vocal proponent of his theory in spite of the lack of following and the objections from the mainstream scholarship.

---

[71] Bianchi: The Language of Qoheleth, 219.

[72] Archer: The Linguistic Evidence, 180.

[73] He argues that, "...there is every reason to deduce from this the suitability of the language of Ecclesiastes to a genre cultivated among the Phoenician-speaking people and adopted from them by a gifted tenth century Hebrew author, composing in a dialect of Canaanite (namely Hebrew) very closely related to Phoenician itself." *Ibid.*, 181.

[74] Seow: Linguistic Evidence, 657.

The Relative Consensus

Gordis championed the third opinion which became a majority view in the following decades. He had defended his position against these two theories. Also, Gordis' view was held in high respect due to its affinity to the colossal reputation of Delitzsch.[75] Barton and Gordis have taken Delitzsch's suggestions to progress their research on the language of Qoheleth.

A consensus was looming as scholars began to identify with the stance of Gordis. So after the emergence and rejection of two theories, the views of Delitzsch still held its ground through the genius and research acumen of proponents like Gordis. Except Whitley who preferred an unreasonably late date,[76] others began to place Qoheleth from the end of the Persian period and till the third century. In spite of the debate on the exact pinpointing of the date, the language of Qoheleth was generally supposed to be late.

The Second Phase: The Resurgence of the Debate

This consensus, which was reached during the 1950s, was suspected by the Jewish scholar named Elyoenai.[77] However,

---

[75] Delitzsch held that, "Qoheleth is connected, yet loosely, with the old language, but at the same time it is in full accord with that New Hebrew we meet in the Mishna..." Delitzsch, *Ecclesiastes*, 190.

[76] Probably Whitley is the only scholar to date Qoheleth after Ben Sira. This view didn't find much following as the *terminus ante quem* was arrived by the discovery of the two Qumran MSS (4QQoh^a and 4Qooh^b), which was dated to the second quarter of the second century BCE. Seow: Linguistic Evidence, 643.

[77] Schoors summarizes the views of Elyoenai: "Qoheleth used an early non-literary popular language and he [Elyoenai] rejects Aramaic as well as Greek influence on that language... he also rejects the idea that Qoheleth's language would represent a transitional stage between BH and MH. In his opinion, it is the language of the end of the First

his works (which are in Hebrew) are not well-known among the English scholarship. In the western scholarship, Soggin observed the impossibility of dating Qoheleth to a late date, based on the linguistic argument.[78] In spite of such observations, a comprehensive analysis of Qoheleth's language had not yet been done.

More specifically, the second phase of the debate commenced after the publication of the books by Isaksson and Fredericks. While Isaksson's doctoral dissertation affirmed that the verbal structure of Qoheleth is mainly BH, Fredericks called for the total reassessment of the linguistic data. In fact, the conclusions of Fredericks were seen as a serious threat to the consensus. Schoors stood up to the challenge to defend the consensus. And the non-chronological interpretation proposed by Young also created quite a stir. Thus, the debate on the language of Qoheleth resumed with greater intensity.

Current Research Trends

In the current research on the language of Qoheleth, the translation theory and the Canaanite-Phoenician theory are completely abandoned. Also, the relative consensus of 1950s has now been seriously challenged by Isaksson, Fredericks and Young. While Isaksson had only questioned the theory of MH's closeness to Qoheleth's language, Fredericks has called the entire premise invalid and supports 8th BCE dating. Young has favored a pre-exilic date for Qoheleth. However, this still remains as a 'minority view.'

Temple Period with few later forms and words which have been wrongly inserted afterwards..." Quoted by Schoors, *Pleasing Words I*, 12.

[78] Alberto Soggin, *Introduction to the Old Testament: From Its Origins to the Closing of the Alexandrian Canon*, trans., John Bowden, (Brescia: Paideia Editrice, 1989), 462-463. Also See, Young, *Diversity*, 140-141.

Most of the modern critical scholarship prefers a late (Hellenistic) date for Qoheleth and understands its language to have Aramaisms and Mishnaisms and to be in close proximity with MH. This view has recently been supported by Schoors, Hurvitz and others in mainstream scholarship. However, the proposal of Young that Biblical texts cannot be dated linguistically and that the Hebrew of LBH literature also resembles some of the EBH books, that they cannot be dated only based on their language has attracted much attention in the recent times.[79]

SUMMARY OF THE CHAPTER

Although Didymus The Blind and Luther pondered the non-Solomonic authorship of Qoheleth, it was Grotius' observation that set the stage for the modern critical scholarship to opt for non-Solomonic preference. Since Grotius, more scholars began to notice and affirm the later date and perceived various traits of Qoheleth's language as chronologically late. The proponents of non-Solomonic authorship found their consummate support from F. Delitzsch who summarized his predecessors' research and defended the non-Solomonic authorship in a most convincing way. He ascribed the language of Qoheleth to be closer to Mishnaic Hebrew. His work greatly redefined the landscape of the future scholarship.

Once the language was considered to be late, scholars began to hypothesize the reason for its lateness and the various influences were perceived in the language. It spawned two major theories: Aramaic translation theory and Canaanite-Phoenician influence theory. In the ensuing centuries, these theories were well objected and rejected by Gordis and others.

---

[79] Ian Young, quoted by Zinoy Zevit, "Symposium Discussion Session: An Edited Transcription," *HS* 46 (2005), 374.

Once again, it was re-established that the language of Qoheleth is closer to the language of Mishnaic period. There was a relative consensus for a few decades.

Again, the debate was reignited by the dissertation of Isaksson, who argued based on the verbal structure that the language of Qoheleth, is distant from Mishnaic Hebrew. Another influential work by Fredericks also challenged the consensus and claimed an 8th century BCE date for Qoheleth. Schoors, Fox, Hurvitz, Joosten and Seow have not accepted these conclusions. While most of them held that the language points to 3rd century, Seow holds that it belongs to the Persian period, still acknowledging the lateness of the language of Qoheleth.

The latest argument to enter the debate belongs to Ian Young. He argues that Qoheleth cannot be considered late based on the language and explains the peculiar features of the languages as being influenced by diglossia, author's style, etc. He perceives that Qoheleth cannot be dated linguistically alone. So in the view of current scholarship, there is no consensus concerning the language of Qoheleth and its date remains unsettled.

2

Recent Studies on the Language of Qoheleth

The former chapter reviewed the development of the linguistic argument. This chapter continues the investigation and sets out to summarize and analyze the major studies pertaining the language of Qoheleth since 19087. This chapter also presents objective evaluations of these major studies. This sets the stage for the final chapter and conclusions.

BO ISAKSSON, STUDIES IN THE LANGUAGE OF QOHELETH, 1987

After the tumultuous decades of tussling with the radical theories, Qoheleth scholarship placidly, with slight objection from the conservative scholarship,[1] settled on the post-exilic/

---

[1] Except G. L. Archer (1969), no other conservative scholar argued for the early date of Qoheleth from the linguistic perspective. However, Archer's views were not well-accepted as he supported the theory of Dahood (i.e., The Canaanite-Phoenician Theory) to arrive at his conclusions. Had he defended the views of Gordis successfully using a different linguistic approach, the trajectory of the scholarly studies could have been different.

Hellenistic date for the Book of Qoheleth. In this context, it was the work of Isaksson that set out to destabilize this consensus. Isaksson's doctoral dissertation from the University of Uppsala, Sweden examined the linguistic premises on which the consensus of the majority Qoheleth scholarship, that the language of Qoheleth points to a later date, was established. His dissertation titled, "Studies in the Language of Qoheleth: With Special Emphasis on the Verbal System" not only questioned this consensus, but also instigated a wave of linguistic studies, specifically focused on the language of Qoheleth in the subsequent years.

Methodology

Isaksson primarily studies the verbal forms in Qoheleth 'to deliver the stagnancy in the Qoheleth's language studies since the discovery of Qumran scrolls.'[2] He notes, "The structural approach achieves paramount importance when dealing with the Semitic verbal system.... In the present work, the structural approach will therefore be apparent mainly in my studies of the verbal system of Qoheleth."[3] Isaksson uses the structural linguistic approach, a synchronic methodology,[4] as proposed by Saussure and developed later by F. Rundgren, his mentor.[5]

---

[2] *Ibid.*, 42.

[3] *Ibid.*, 23.

[4] John Barton, *Reading the Old Testament*, 16. Barton terms it as one of the "Text-imminent" approaches.

[5] The classic text book (French: *Cours de linguistique générale*) defining the Saussurean theory of structural linguistics was published posthumously in 1916. See, Ferdinand de Saussure, R. Harris (trans. by), *Course in General Linguistic* (Paris: Open Court Publishing company, 2006). In which Saussure argues, "The linguist must take the study of linguistic structure as his primary concern, and relate all other manifestations of language to it." *Ibid.*, 9.

Isaksson is so far the only biblical linguist to have applied structural linguistics to Qoheleth Studies.

He points out that Qoheleth is a product of one historical time and one social community, and so the verbal system of Qoheleth has to be identified with the verbal system of his time and his community.[6] However, the difference between the community and the author relates to the spoken aspect of language (*la parole*) and not to the structure of the language itself (*la langue*). Isaksson, following Rundgren, observes that, "in proto-Semitic verbal systems, an opposition between the idea of motion and change (FIENS) and stativity (STATIVE) has been expressed grammatically in the oppositions *qatal* (Suffix Conjugation) and *yaqtul* (Prefix Conjugation)."[7] PC has two values in *la langue*: "one neutral, expressing an indifference towards the marks of stativity, and another negative, expressing the opposite to the stative idea, i.e., motion, change."[8] Structural linguistics views language as composed by signs which is characterized *la langue*[9] (system of language in a community) and *la parole*[10] (speech of individuals). These signs have two

---

[6] Authors do not invent language, rather they formulates their texts based on the existing linguistic structures which are at their disposal from their immediate community. *Ibid.*, 17.

[7] *Ibid.*, 25

[8] *Ibid.*, 25

[9] Structuralists believe that "language is a social phenomenon that doesn't permit the author to create a language of his own ... it's not a matter of an individual's choice..." If Qoheleth lived in a community, his language was uttered in the context of his community. It is known as *la langue*. *Ibid.*, 17.

[10] *La parole* is explained as "that which is individual, and hence what is special and characteristic for a specific text in the same community." It points to the fact that the verbal system of the Qoheleth text was the verbal system of his time in his community. *Ibid.*, 17

aspects which are known as *Signifiant*[11] (Signifier) and *Signifie*[12] (Signified). Also, it claims that language should be understood as a set of signs in opposition.[13] Two types of comparisons in *la langue*: paradigmatic (associative) and Syntagmatic[14] which governs the structure of the text. He outlines the earlier seminal studies and their deficiencies in approaching the Hebrew verbs. So on these premises, he begins his study on the verbs in Qoheleth.

Summary and Analysis

In his introduction, Isaksson summarizes structural linguistics approach and how it'd be applied to Qoheleth. Isaksson states his methodology that the structure of the language (*la langue*) is conservative to change compared to the spoken language (*la parole*). So he sets out to study the aspects of SC (*qatal*) and PC

---

[11] Isaksson defines it as "sound image" which is a psychological entity, being the mental picture of a series of phonemes, carrying the concept in an indissoluble union. *Ibid.*, 11-12.

[12] The concept with which the sound image is associated with is *signifie*. If *signifiant* is the mental concept, the *signifie* is an actual object in the world, or the memory of the image that is evoked in one's mind when hearing the sound. *Ibid.*, 11.

[13] de Saussure: "a linguistic system is a series of sound differences combined with a series of conceptual differences." *Ibid.*, 12.

[14] In the study of the sign process (Semiotics), it points to the analysis of syntax as opposed to paradigms. See also, Saussure, *Course*, 121-125. While Syntagmatic relation is built upon the linear nature of language (in the syntax), the Paradigmatic relation is connected with brain to make associations in the mind. This associative ability helps one to analyze the syntagms. Syntagms are segments within the text; it could consist of words, group of words or whole sentences. Sentences and phrases are called as complex types of syntagms. *Ibid.*, 13. There are diverse syntagmatic forms: sequential, spatial and conceptual. Mostly texts contain more than one type of syntagmatic structure with one dominant type. See, *http://www.aber.ac.uk/media/Documents/S4B/sem04.html* (Accessed on August 12, 2009).

(*yaktul*) which expresses the idea of motion in Hebrew/Semitic verbal systems in the *la langue*. He observes that "in the case of BH, no one can rely on a native speaker competence" and moves on to criticize two native Israeli scholars: Talmy Givon had failed "to note the ample usage of the PC for the gnomic present in the proverbial statements of the Old Testament" and also disregarding "the crucial distinction between the nominal and verbal clauses."[15] Isaksson observes that Amnon Gordon wrongly presupposed that 'the verbal forms in [Classical Hebrew] have an inherent reference to time" and he too disregards the distinction between nominal/verbal clauses.[16] Isaksson concludes that both of these scholars proceed to their conclusions not directed by sound linguistic principles, rather by their *sens linguistique* (language sense) of Israeli Hebrew. He also underlines his intension while stating "our notion of the (finite) verb becomes decisive when we are to discuss the function of the participle in the verbal system."[17]

On the verbal usage in the auto-biographical narrations of Qoheleth, he identifies 'all the 1cs verb forms that refer to

---

[15] Talmy Givon, *Verb complements and Relative Clauses: A Diachronic case study in Biblical Hebrew* (Malibu, CA:1974). The purpose of his study was to pinpoint the departure point from VSO to SVO in BH. He used lamentations, Ecclesiastes and Song of Songs as his test cases in which he studied the functions of PC, SC and the participle. *Ibid.*, 37.

[16] Gordon concludes his research on participles: "it is clear then that I regard the nominal aspect of the participle as the main reason for the preponderance of SVO order in sentences with participles; I claim that the participle functions as a predicate nominal and predicate nominals follow the subject in Hebrew, Biblical and Mishnaic and Modern." Amnon Gordon, *The development of the participle in Biblical, Mishnaic and Modern Hebrew* (Malibu, CA: 1982), 21. Isaksson points out, "regarding the tenses, Givon fails to understand that a verb form may have time references in a given context without any time whatsoever being inherent in the verb form itself." *Ibid.*, 38.

[17] *Ibid.*, 34.

Qoheleth himself / verb forms that are connected with the author' as the autobiographical thread which runs from 1:12 – 10:7.[18] He notes that with few exceptions, "the verb forms used in the autobiographical thread are exclusively SC forms, sometimes preceded by waw."[19] He also observes a gradual shift within the autobiographical narratives, as it moves towards the later chapters, from the *tunc*-level (with reference to the past) to the *nunc*-level (with reference to the present). He identifies this by the recurring use of *hineh* as well as *yes* (existential particle).[20] He also points out the non-occurrence of *waw*-conversive in the SC. He concludes, "A survey of the SC forms in the thread leads to the conclusion that the SC forms preceded by *waw* (wSC) appear to perform exactly the same function as those without *waw*."[21] It functions almost like perfect.[22] He relates the preference to SC, instead of waPC, in Qoheleth to the special character of the book, its philosophical approach which is unique in the Hebrew Bible and the absence of any direct historical narration.[23] He terms this special characteristic as *resumé* and holds that this feature cannot be claimed as late.[24]

In the review of Niphal עשה in Qoheleth, he observes that "all the *niphal* forms (except 8:11) follow immediately after a

---

[18] He lists total 81 SC forms: without *waw* (61x) and preceded by *waw* (21x). He uses charts to show the distribution of SC forms in the autobiographical thread.

[19] Ibid., 43

[20] Ibid., 45-47.

[21] Based on this observation, he objects the Frequentative Theory (it sees Aramaic influence on wSC) which claims that a SC form preceded by *waw* undergoes a kind of conversion and takes on the nature of the PC. Ibid., 56-57.

[22] Ibid., 69.

[23] Ibid., 61.

[24] Ibid., 55.

relative pronoun and in all these cases the "activity" is clearly stated to be "under the sun", "under the heaven" or "on earth."[25] He lists three possibilities for translations and prefers the third: 1) here the "works" or "actions" in view were finished in the past and so perfect sense should be used; 2) it is viewed as ongoing and present in the "now" of the autobiographical narration, however not viewed as present to the author's now; 3) it meant to be valid in the now of the author (and the reader). He concludes that "the forms of עשה Nifal refer to activities, or an activity that goes on in the present of the author, "under the sun."[26]

Isaksson also explores the usage of SC as a form used to express action in the present, more often a gnomic present. [27] He examines 20 cases to illustrate this point.[28] He observes the function of SC as "general or stative present" in the linguistic community of Qoheleth. Then he goes on to conclude that "at the time the book was created the SC category had not yet been temporalized. In several cases the archaic stative value of the SC may be observed."[29] He further examines the twenty seven instances of the wSC outside the autobiographical thread.[30] And

---

[25] Ibid., 70.

[26] Ibid., 74. He doesn't prefer perfect to translate *na'asa*.

[27] Wallace's definition of gnomic present is well-explanatory: "Gnomic present may be used to make a statement of a general timeless fact. It doesn't say that something is happening, but that something does happen. The action or state continues without time limits. The verb is used in proverbial statements or general maxims about what occurs at all times." See, Daniel B. Wallace, *Greek Grammar Beyond the Basics: An Exegetical Syntax of the New Testament*, (Grand Rapids: Zondervan, 1996), 523.

[28] 1:9,1:12, 2:18, 2:23,2:26, 3:11, 3:14, 3:15a, 4:3, 5:10, 5:17,6:3, 6:10, 7:10, 7:14, 7:19, 7:24, 7:27-28, 8:15, 9:9.

[29] Ibid., 92.

[30] The wSC forms outside the thread: 1:5 (2), 2:24 (2), 3:13 (2), 4:11, 5:5, 5:13 (2), 5:18, 9:14-15 (5x), 10:3, 12:1, 12:2, 12:3 (3), 12:4, 12:5, 12:6,

he concludes that in addition to the *resumé* function, the specific usage of the SC in conjunctive position (commonly known as 'perfect consecutive' or 'converted perfect') is an undeniable syntactical reality in the language of Qoheleth.[31]

He examines eight verbs that are "sufficiently frequent and have sufficiently differentiated application."[32] His investigation mainly focuses on the finite forms of the verb as well as the predicative and indefinite occurrences of the participle. He observes the nature of BH verbal forms in general and in Qoheleth in particular. Also each verbs are examined based on their SC, PC and Participle functions in Qoheleth. Isaksson makes few observations: "when actuality is to be expressed in BH, the PC is normally the very form being used;"[33] "in general, the stative value of the SC is realized either as a general present or as a perfect;"[34] "In Qoheleth, a participle of this verb seems to express a property of human person, that is, so to speak inherent in his conditions of life. It expresses something constitutional;"[35] "the basic nature of PC is actuality and this value of the category may have been the decisive factor in the choice of verb from here [in 11:5 and 8:7];"[36] "as can be seen at many places in the book (8:26, 9:9, etc), the SC form following

---

12:9 (2x). Out of these, only 7 instances have resume type function: 9:14-15 (5x) and 12:9 (2x). See, *Ibid.*, 93.

[31] This view is opposite to that of M. Dahood who held that "there's no converted perfect with the waw in Qoheleth." Isaksson responds, saying "this is not true... there are such examples and considering the character and size of the book, they cannot even be few. *Ibid.*, 105.

[32] He says studying one semantheme at a time is the ideal method of studying verbs. *Ibid.*, 16.

[33] *Ibid.*, 108.

[34] *Ibid.*, 110.

[35] *Ibid.*, 113.

[36] *Ibid.*, 116.

a relative pronoun may be used for the gnomic present."[37] He finds that the usage of PC in Qoheleth is the same as in classical BH.[38]

Chapters, seven to nine, present the conclusion of Isaksson's analysis of the verbal system in Qoheleth.[39] He finds that the Prefix conjugation is closer to BH in general. He also observes some special cases which are not reported in BH:[40] waPC is infrequent, to that Isaksson evokes the "Philosophical and sapiental character of the book" to explain this anomaly. The following chapter concludes the findings on "Active verbal participle."[41] The main question this chapter seeks to answer is "is it possible to detect any finite nuance of the participle in the text of Qoheleth?" He only notes one case in 7:26.[42] Isaksson observes, "This usage of the participle [in 7:26] comes to rather close to the use of the participle in the spoken language of

---

[37] Ibid., 124.

[38] Ibid., 130.

[39] The chapters are titled as follows: The Prefix Conjugation (Chapter 7), The Active Participle (Chapter 8) and The Verbal System in Qoheleth – summary (Chapter 9).

[40] PC after interrogative pronoun *mi*. He observes "the phrase mi + PC form is exclusively used in qoheleth to formulate a rhetorical question, beginning with "who will..." or "who would..." as in 6:12 Ibid., 133.

[41] He takes the requirements of participle given by K. Eksell: it should be a) a predicate, b) indefinite, c) for the transitive verbs, able to take an objectival and not a genitival complement. But Isaksson thinks that the third condition somehow implies the native speaker acquaintance to pinpoint such function for the verb. He is critical of the third point here: "I even doubt that such a requirement is advisable since it relies entirely on the surface structure of the language." Ibid., 134.

[42] Other cases, he considers participles as close to verbal adjectives in predicative position. Ibid., 135. He also observes, its [participle] actual verbal usage is yet too specialized, or restricted to individual semanthemes. Ibid., 141.

classical BH."[43] Based on this observation, Isaksson concludes, "this is one more indication that the idiom of Qoheleth in many respects comes closer to the spoken language than the standard narrative Hebrew." [44] Also he takes the participle in gnomic sense and not as actual present tense as used sometimes in the direct speeches of CH.[45] He also summarizes the study for easy reference, with a number of observations: SC in Qoheleth is used in relatively restricted varieties of applications,[46] the use of participle is well within the range of CH,[47] PC is used in a way that is normal in BH.[48] In the *nunc* [Present] level:[49] SC is stative or general present; PC is actual cursive present/ generalized present with an actual or factual nuance/ gnomic present; Participle is general or gnomic. In the *tunc* [Past] level:[50] SC is a neutralized constative aspect, often realized as perfect/ time determined by *kebar*. PC sometimes expresses a neutralized constative aspect; participle not used in *tunc* level.

Isaksson also discusses other grammatical aspects such as pronouns, adverbs of existence and negation and study of ōlām

---

[43] He agrees with T. Muraoka here, "the pattern PREDICATE-PARTICIPLE + SUBJECT is fairly frequent in the conversational style of Judges and 1 Samuel, while it is very infrequent in the narrative of the same books, and totally absent in the legal language." *Ibid.*, 138.

[44] *Ibid.*, 138.

[45] Isaksson concludes as follows: "Thus I regard the clauses involved as nominal... uses that probably were characteristic of spoken Hebrew in biblical, also early biblical times." *Ibid.*, 139.

[46] He also observes, "SC/wSC have similar functions in Qoheleth... I have not been able to find instances of the constative aspect in relevance position (punctual aspect), not the so-called case of co-incidence." *Ibid.*, 140.

[47] *Ibid.*, 140

[48] *Ibid.*, 140.

[49] *Ibid.*, 141.

[50] *Ibid.*, 141.

in 3:11. Chapter ten expounds on the pronouns of Qoheleth: independent personal pronouns (הֵמָּה, הִיא, הוּא, אַתְּ, אַתָּה, אֲנִי),[51] demonstrative pronoun (the use of definite article, זֶה and זֹה, הַהוּא, אֵלֶּה),[52] relative pronouns (אֲשֶׁר, שֶׁ, שׁ),[53] interrogative pronouns (מִי, מַה, מֶה, לָמָּה, בַּמֶּה, אֵי־זֶה),[54] indefinite pronouns (כֻּלָּם / בַּכֹּל / לַכֹּל / הַכֹּל / כָּל / כֹּל, מְאוּמָה).[55] Then he studies the pronoun אֲנִי and the SC, in which he argues that the

---

[51] He observes that the longer form 'anôkî is not used in Qoheleth. He suggests that it may be a characteristic of northern Hebrew dialect. *Ibid.*, 142-144.

[52] The definite article occurs 381 times in Qoheleth. But its usage is very unpredictable. Zimmermann has raised the question: "why do we have within the same sentence, within the same phrase, nouns in a series, sometimes with, sometimes without the article, sometime needlessly and indiscriminately added, sometime inexplicably dropped?" He explained this feature as due to the Aramaic Translation, and Dahood explained it in terms of Phoenician influence. Isaksson points out this issue and suggests that certain poetical freedom in the use of article must be allowed, since Qoheleth contains both poetry and sayings of a proverbial character. However, he also acknowledges that the issue is still enigmatic and doesn't propose any definite solutions. *Ibid.*, 145-148. Also the classical Hebrew demonstrative pronoun *zoth* doesn't occur in Qoheleth.

[53] Isaksson points out that the usage of אֲשֶׁר (89x - 57%) and שֶׁ (67x - 43%). And out of this usage, they have relative usage for 42 times each. He observes that in MH, שֶׁ is used exclusively, except for the direct quotations from the Hebrew bible. But, the Qumran texts have only two attested instances of שֶׁ usage, אֲשֶׁר dominates there. However, in conclusion, Isaksson prefers to see the influence of northern Hebrew dialect, although he doesn't rule out the possibility of Aramaic influence. *Ibid.*, 148-161.

[54] *Ibid.*, 161-162.

[55] Isaksson observes that כֹּל is one of the most common words in Qoheleth (90x). Qoheleth shows highest frequency of among the books of the OT, closely followed by Deuteronomy (353x), Proverb (77x) and Job (73x). It may be due to the philosophical character of the book, containing many general presuppositions on life on earth, as well as the favorite theme of the author: הֲבֵל הֲבָלִים. *Ibid.*, 162-163.

pronouns (especially אֲנִי) cannot be considered as "pleonastic,"[56] rather "the pronoun is added in instances of greater importance, where the narrative halts for a moment to make a conclusion or to introduce a new thought."[57]

Isaksson further discusses four adverbs of existence (יֵשׁ)[58] and negation (אַל (21x), לֹא (65x), אֵין (44x).[59] Here, he points out that the usages of adverbs are within the boundaries of CH grammar. At last, he does the lexical study of the word "הָעֹלָם" in 3:11 which he treats as the *crux interpretum* and it is loosely connected to the earlier study. Qoheleth's search for wisdom ends with this conclusion that no one can perceive the work that is done before and will be done after. And so, Qoheleth advocates a life of contentment, rather than ceaseless vain striving. And the central purpose of such life, according to Isaksson, should be the fear of God.

Conclusions of Isaksson

After a laborious study, Isaksson is modest in his conclusions and he draws out a number of insightful observations: this distinctiveness of Qoheleth's language does not concern the verbal system as much as has often been assumed…the linguistic distance from MH is considerable (194), it is probable that the language the author used for his work was heavily

---

[56] Pleonasm is defined as the use of more words to express an idea, i.e., redundancy.

[57] *Ibid.*, 171.

[58] The existential particle "יֵשׁ" is used most frequently than in any other books of the Old Testament: Qoheleth (16x), Proverbs (13x), Job (12x), Isaiah (2x). Qoheleth uses it to introduce examples of what he has observed under the sun. *Ibid.*, 172-173.

[59] אֵין is used according to the rules of Classical Hebrew. *Ibid.*, 174-175.

influenced by a local dialect, or was a local dialect, closer to the spoken language than was classical narrative Hebrew (196), out of the six features of LBH (as proposed by J. Naveh and J. C. Greenfield), Qoheleth shares only one (196), the grammatical basis is still mainly BH (197), our knowledge of the Hebrew, spoken and written, that was current in the various regions and in the several periods of the Biblical times, is too limited to permit a dating and a geographic location for Qoheleth purely on linguistic grounds (197). He hopes that another discovery of a philosophical-sapiential kind of ancient Hebrew documents might revolutionize studies on Qoheleth's language.

Evaluation of Isaksson

Isaksson's monograph has drawn considerably favorable evaluation among the critical scholarship. It may be due to the mild nature of his conclusion which does not seek to primarily establish any specific dating for the book, rather focused on demonstrating where the verbal system of Qoheleth fits in.[60] His application of structural linguistics to the study of Ecclesiastes has been generally admired. The basic assumption of structuralism establishes the principle that the author does not create his own language and the language changes are not reflected in the structure (*la langue*) as in the presentation (*la parole*). Murphy satirically comments on the opening section of the monograph that describes the methodology as written "in somewhat indigestible jargon that has become characteristic of structuralism."[61] Indeed, it is hard for anyone without a basic

---

[60] Isaksson hesitantly writes, "An origin in the fourth century is by no means improbable, although such a hypothesis does little to solve the problem of geographical and dialectal locality." *Ibid.*, 197.

[61] Roland E. Murphy, "Review of Isaksson," *CBQ* 51 (1989), 333.

knowledge on Structuralism to carefully track the progression of the argument laid.

One of the notable contributions of Isaksson is his identification that the autobiographical-reflective nature of the book is echoed in the structure of the verbal system. In view of the syntax, an array of SC forms in the first person singular, occasionally preceded by *waw* as well as the rarity of waPC reveals such implicit intention.[62] This view is generally accepted into current scholarship.[63]

Isaksson's proposal to translate הָעֹלָם which he recognizes as "the great *crux interpretum* of the book of Qoheleth" as 'eternal work' lies surely beyond his linguistic observations. And Murphy wonders that "it is not clear to me how God has put this into the human heart... if הָעֹלָם means all that [Isaksson] claims, then humans would understand the work of God!"[64] However, the study of the verbal system remains unaffected by the interpretation of this lexical discussion.

And Gammie who reviewed Isaksson in Hebrew Studies points out four areas of Isaksson's study which might require

---

[62] Isaksson writes, "My conclusion is that the choice of conjunctive SC and wSC forms in the autobiographical thread is due to the special kind of narrative that constitutes this thread. The narrative of the thread is of the resume type... There are many examples of this kind of resumé narration from all genres of the Old Testament, which means that this special feature of the book is not a valid proof of lateness. The infrequent usage of waPC forms is noted... My conclusion is that the low frequency of this verbal usage is a matter of literary genre: the philosophical approach of the book and the absence of straightforward historical narration." See, Isaksson, *Studies in the Language of Qoheleth*, 190.

[63] Craig G. Bartholomew. *Reading Ecclesiastes: Old Testament Exegesis and Hermeneutical Theory*, 151.

[64] Murphy, "Review of Isaksson," 333.

modification or supplementation.[65] However, his overall assessment of Isaksson's work is positive; he states, "In the current volume Isaksson has, among other things, shown convincingly that the verbal system of Qoheleth remains at quite a distance from MH."[66] His work is along with the erudition, more objective methodology and carefully researched linguistic details would be remembered, if not for anything else, for his conclusion that at best questioned the *communis opinio* that the language of Qoheleth is closer to MH.

DANIEL C. FREDERICKS, QOHELETH'S LANGUAGE: RE-EVALUATING ITS NATURE AND DATE, 1988

Closely after the publication of Isaksson's dissertation, Daniel C. Fredericks published his highly provocative book on the language of Qoheleth.[67] It totally upset the *sensus communis* about its late post-exilic dating for Qoheleth. Whereas Isaksson had only pointed out that the verbal structure of Qoheleth remains closer to BH than to MH, Fredericks conclusions were straight forward and pointed to a definite dating to pre-exilic period. Fredericks work called for the total reassessment of the

---

[65] Gammie presents four criticisms: 1) possible use of *waw* as a subordinating conjunction in 5:5; 2) analysis of an idiomatic usage of the verb from the non-idiomatic usage; 3) failure to present the reason for the dominant use of SC in Manual 0f Discipline and Qumran and in Qoheleth; 4) the regular use of הָאֱלֹהִים with article might show northern Hebrew dialect in Qoheleth. John G. Gammie, "Review of Isaksson," *Hebrew Studies* 30 (1989), 151. In his response to Gammie's criticisms, Isaksson admits not treating the idiomatic usages of the verbs. He accepted the criticisms gracefully with the exception of the third. See, Bo Isaksson, "Correspondence" *HS* 31 (1990), 276.

[66] John G. Gammie, "Review of Isaksson," 152.

[67] Quite obviously, Isaksson's work was possibly not available to Fredericks for reference, though it was published a year earlier. It's not mentioned in the bibliography either, an inevitable predicament for the authors.

consensus. It was a daring attempt to go against the strongly-cemented beliefs of the mainstream scholarship. Fredericks' observations, along with the earlier conclusions of Isaksson, have resurrected the debate on the language of Qoheleth and brought to it a renewed intensity. Also, the depth of Fredericks' study makes it imperative for anyone dealing with the language of Qoheleth not to take his work lightly.

Methodology

Fredericks begins the book with a definite purpose, "this study anticipates contributing to that discussion by assessing previous methods, arguments, and conclusions, and by working through the language in a comparative approach to discover more accurate description of the language and its implication on dating Qoheleth."[68]

Fredericks employs a methodology which includes the four primary components: grammar and vocabulary, genre and a plausible dialectal influence. As far as the grammatical-lexical comparisons, he perceives, "Linguistic comparison of literature should entail primarily the grammar and syntax of the text, its lexical character only secondarily."[69] He recognizes the influence of genre in assessing Qoheleth's language accurately, for "Qoheleth is the only extant Hebrew work of its kind, and one might expect its language to reflect a certain degree of singularity."[70]

---

[68] Fredericks, *Qoheleth's Language*, 1.

[69] *Ibid.*, 28.

[70] Similar observations have also been made by the earlier scholars Delitzsch, Gordis, Segal, supposing Qoheleth might be the first work of this kind. Though Fredericks calls this 'a weak supposition,' he appreciates their appliance of such assumption into their linguistic treatment of Qoheleth. *Ibid.*, 28.

He also considers the North Israelite dialectal influence in the language of Qoheleth, and calls for the re-examination of the view that these peculiar features point to later date. It might be the influence of dialect or vernacular element in the language. He thinks that, "this vernacular element should be seriously considered in any comprehensive study of the language, and should be given due attention as a main cause for its unique linguistic character."[71] With these methodological observations and delineations, Fredericks begins his elaborate study on the language of Qoheleth.

Summary and Analysis

This book, Qoheleth's Language, contains seven chapters, including introduction, conclusion and the implication for further research. There are four major chapters: first two major chapters trace the history of the development of linguistic argument, various theories and outline his methodological approach and purpose of this study, the following two major chapters get into the deeper study of the language under two major categories: grammatical comparisons and lexical comparisons.

In the introduction, Fredericks surveys the factors which were considered in determining the date of Qoheleth in the earlier scholarship: possible Greek influence, historical allusions, monotheism in Qoheleth as a pointer to the late date, skepticism as the result of the destruction of temple and exile, Qoheleth's usage of earlier biblical works, poor and unaesthetic language style, linguistic features of Qoheleth as pointer to later date.[72] He points out that with the discovery of Qumran

---

[71] *Ibid.*, 43.

[72] Perdue in his recent book "Sword and Stylus" prefers a Ptolomic period dating for Qoheleth. See, Leo G. Perdue, *The Sword and The Stylus: An Introduction to Wisdom in the Age of Empires* (Grand Rapids:

manuscripts (4QQoh^a), the *terminus ante quem* was proposed by Muilenburg and accepted generally.[73] However, Whitley dated Qoheleth to 152-145 BCE, whose view was not accepted by the mainstream scholarship. While other approaches were proven to be controversial, Qoheleth scholarship turned to language studies.[74]

Fredericks reviews the three major theories that flabbergasted the scholarly world in the 20th century, and then unfolds the purpose of his study. He summarizes and analyzes the claims of the three theories: Mishnaic Hebrew and The Aramaic Influence Theory, Aramaic Translation Theory, Canaanite- Phoenician Influence Theory. Mishnaic and Aramaic influence theory, was proposed by Delitzsch (1875), developed and advocated by Barton (1908), Gordis (1968) and others, and recently advocated by Whitley (1978).[75] He rejects the grammatical as well as lexical analysis of Dahood, Zimmerman and Whitley.[76] According to him, the peculiar features of the language are the result of native Hebrew

---

Eerdmans, 2008), 201. The succession of three kings in 4:13-16 is referred often to validate this line of thought. Hertzberg and Lohfink views the instructions of loyalty in 8:2ff to fit the time of the Ptolomies and Seleucids. Fredericks, *Qoheleth's Language*, 4-5.

[73] J. Muilenburg, "A Qoheleth Scroll from Qumran," *BASOR 135* (1954): 20-28. F. M. Cross, "The Oldest Manuscripts from Qumran," *JBL 74* (1955): 153-162.

[74] Fredericks observes, "the weight of Qoh's date has rested typically more on the linguistic phenomena than any other." Fredericks, *Qoheleth's Language*, 7.

[75] Whitley's commentary was taken as the latest representative of Mishnaic Hebrew and Aramaic Influence Theory, as it was published, ten years before the publication of Fredericks' book.

[76] Fredericks also notes that "Qoheleth presents a comprehensive picture of the way the article may be used or not used, according to BH principles." Cf. *Ibid.*, 15, 17. Dahood prefers to translate b as 'from', not 'in / into' as often rendered.

idiosyncrasies and possible indication of Northern Hebrew element in the language. Then he outlines the purpose of his study as "to re-examine the evidence and the underlying premises (of scholarly consensus), because there are obvious superficialities and inadequacies at various points."[77] He sees his purpose as "not to settle the question of Qoheleth's date, but to contribute to the decision process that includes the nature of its language as a primary datum."[78]

Fredericks delineates his "General Methodological Concerns," which is mainly focused on grammatical-lexical comparisons. He uses a separate chapter to outline his methodology "in order to indicate the direction of the argument, and to provide a framework for the detailed data that follow in the fourth (grammatical comparisons) and fifth chapters (lexical comparisons)."[79] Here, he emphasizes the importance of the awareness of the genre as well as the north Israelite/vernacular dialect along with the grammatical-lexical comparisons.

Fredericks further compares the Qoheleth with Mishnaic Hebrew (MH), Second Temple Hebrew (STH) as well as Late Biblical Hebrew (LBH). His grammatical comparisons with MH are mainly based on the Segal's grammar.[80] Also, Fredericks notes the difficulties of finding standard MH manuscripts, as observed by Kutscher.[81] But he continues "there is no reason

---

[77] Fredericks, *Qoheleth's Language*, 24.

[78] *Ibid.*, 24.

[79] *Ibid.*, 27.

[80] M. A. Segal, *A Grammar of Mishnaic Hebrew* (Oxford: Clarendon Press, 1927).

[81] Kutscher explained "it can be shown that during the Middle ages the copyists, and later the printers, tried to harmonize the MH with BH... this correction tendency led to a complete distortion of the linguistic structure of MH." Kutscher, 1964, 35f.

to be believe that a reconstructed grammar of MH would be any more similar to Qoh's language than MH is now believed to be."[82] This way, he finds it reasonable to use Segal's book for his grammatical comparisons.

The section on Mishnaic Hebrew and Qoheleth is subdivided into three categories: Method, Evidence and Summary. And Evidence is further sorted into three groups: verb, noun and pronoun. Fredericks investigates 61 cases of possible MH influence.[83] He uses five principles to guide his study of 61 cases: Exclusively MH, Equally BH and MH, More Characteristics of MH (a. Independent of MH; b. Dependent on MH), More Characteristic of BH and Neither BH nor MH.[84] Then, Fredericks undertakes the comprehensive study of the verbs, nouns and pronouns. Analysis of the verbs under stem as well as aspects goes into painstaking details. He reiterates that the verbal foundation is more characteristic of BH. The verbal stems are analyzed under 14 categories.[85] In each instances, Fredericks comes to the conclusion that the stems are more in proximity with BH. Also, he contrasts the usage of plene with other defectives and concludes the rarity of its occurrences in Qoheleth is well in line with BH.[86] While

---

[82] *Ibid.*, 52.

[83] Fredericks notes the rationale for his choice of 61 words as "either because they are said to be grammatical properties which show Qoheleth's dependence on MH or because they offer differences between BH and MH that allow Qoh to align with BH or MH in a given category." *Ibid.*, 52.

[84] *Ibid.*, 52-53.

[85] Qal orthography, Piel orthography, Pual orthography, Pual overall frequency, Pual finite aspect' frequency, Poel frequency, Poal frequency, Hithpoel frequency, Pilpel frequency, Hophal frequency, Niphal infinitive with lamed, Niphal morphology, Hithpael frequency, Hithpael passive, and Nithpael.

[86] *Ibid.*, 54.

analyzing the aspects: perfect and imperfect, he answers number of claims which are made for Qoheleth's lateness: Qoheleth uses perfect to convey present, a function that is completely absent in MH; a claim that perfect *waw* consecutive is absent in Qoheleth is shown to be wrong by the listing of 16 *waw* consecutive perfects; imperfective was used as subjunctive in MH but has fuller range of usage as present, future and subjunctive; absence of imperfect as cohortatives in MH but Qoheleth uses it, etc. He also makes two perceptive observations on the translation of the aspects.[87] He undertakes a detailed study on Infinitive Constructs and Absolutes which brings him to see them as more characteristic of BH.[88] He also presents a well-balanced study on the participles in Qoheleth.[89] He classifies them under 'Equally BH and MH'[90] as well as More Characteristic of MH.[91] Other verbal conjugations are said to be either BH and MH or more characteristic of BH, nothing

---

[87] Fredericks makes two suggestions: 1) when Qoh wished to describe an act or thought as simple past (preterite), he added *'anî* to the conjugated perfect, thus referring to his specific quest (1:16, 2:1, 2:11-15, 17, 18, 20, 24, 3:16-18, 5:17, 7:25,8:15, 9:16. Also see, Daniel 10:7, 12:5, Cant 5:5, 6, 2 Sam 17:15). 2) Qoh avoids the consecutive imperfect with *waw* possibly because its use would only have led to temporal and logical ambiguity. He further thinks that the *waw* consecutive imperfect is typical of historical narratives and thus not necessary to be used in Qoheleth. Here he sees the bearing of genre playing a major role. *Ibid.*, 78-82.

[88] Except one case which he sees as "Equally BH and MH" - Infinitive absolute as an emphatic cognate with the finite verb. *Ibid.*, 85.

[89] The use of participles in Qoheleth is within the accepted function of the participle in BH and they were used in BH to express statements of general truth. *Ibid.*, 87-88.

[90] Participle as Present Tense, Participle with Pronominal subject, and Participle with Pronominal subject and *'aein* – as Equally BH and MH. *Ibid.*, 86-90.

[91] Participle in semi-conditional clauses, participle orthography: masculine plural – More characteristic of BH. *Ibid.*, 91.

actually showing any extreme affinity with MH. In the subsequent study on the nouns, Fredericks sees that duplications are also found in BH and are not exclusive to MH,[92] mutual substitution of masculine and feminine nouns are found also in BH in 118 instances.[93] Also the other features of nouns such as genitive expression as well as anticipatory suffix are shown to be more characteristic of BH.[94] And the usages of the pronouns are shown to be not closer to MH exclusively. He concludes his study of Mishnaic Hebrew and Qoheleth with the quotation of Greenfield which shows his conviction as well.[95]

The following section compares the Second Temple Hebrew (STH) with Qoheleth. Here Fredericks takes Ben Sira, Copper Scroll, Bar Kosiba Letters, Qumran scrolls to compare the features that are different from the BH. Whitley held that BS predates Qoheleth, citing grammatical features, like Qoheleth's use of prepositional *lamed*. But Fredericks explains it as follows: "to employ lamed as a preposition to the indirect object after

---

[92] Fredericks renders the argument of Whitley that the duplicated nominal pattern in Qoh 12:5 is evidence of the Mishnaic character of Qoheleth's language, as an inaccurate generalization. *Ibid.*, 94-95

[93] Here, Fredericks lists the six examples given by Sigfried as related to the MH feature of forming feminine nouns from masculine BH nouns and vice-versa. However, Fredericks cites the study of A. Sperber who lists 118 cases where the masculine and feminine forms of the noun exist. *Ibid.*, 96. He observes that the plural of *pardesim* is in line with BH morphology.

[94] *Ibid.*, 96-97.

[95] Greenfield already questioned this conclusion: "...the proposition that the Hebrew of Koheleth is a middle stage between late biblical Hebrew and Mishnaic Hebrew containing many Aramaisms, has little to recommend... why is the syntax of Koheleth on the whole so different from Mishnaic Hebrew?" Quoted by Fredericks, *Qoheleth's Language*, 109.

אמר, is natural Hebrew even as early as Gen 41:55E, Exo 3:14E, 2 Sam 7:8."[96] The rarity of *waw* consecutives which are taken as the pointer of lateness is also refuted.[97] Again, the usage of relative particle also is within the range of BH.[98] Fredericks is severe in his criticism on Whitley's position:

> "In summary, when it comes to Qoh and Ben Sira, Whitley's grammatical argument is very weak since apart from his critical errors in reciting basic evidence, he fails to take into account alternate explanations. Still the additional weakness in his grammatical assessment is that he allows at most 20 years for these grammatical distinctions to develop... in other words, developments that Hebrew scholars and grammarians describe in centuries, Whitley contracts to two decades or less."[99]

He also shows some grammatical traits in Ben Sira which are more frequent in MH than in BH.[100] Here, Fredericks convincingly shows that the language of Qoheleth is more in line with BH than with Ben Sira and STH. Also eight grammatical traits in Qoh compared with the Hebrew of the Copper scroll and the Bar Koshiba letters with Qoheleth.[101]

---

[96] *Ibid.*, 113.

[97] Fredericks notes that "the *waw* consecutive perfects are not absent in Qoh. They occur frequently – at least 16 times." *Ibid.*, 114.

[98] Whitley holds that *še* is absent in BS. But Fredericks shows that it is present more than 16 times. See, *Ibid.*, 114.

[99] *Ibid.*, 115.

[100] Some of the grammatical categories that are discussed: mutual substitution of masculine and feminine nouns (Qoh has one but BS has five cases), mutual substitution of singular and plural nouns (Qoh has no instances, BS has 5 cases), verbal nouns (Qoh has 1 disputed case, but BS has 11 cases), the infinitive construct with preposition, preposition-*lamed* as accusative (Qoh no case but BS has it. It is a MH feature according to Segal). *Ibid.*, 115-117.

[101] Both are dated to the first and second CE respectively. The areas that are compared: infinitive construct with preposition, participle as present tense, masculine plural orthography, verbal nouns, genitive - masculine plural orthography, relative particle, *el* for *la*. Each one of

Fredericks writes, "Nothing is unique to these documents and Qoh alone. In fact, all these characteristic are indicative of the difference between BH and MH as well, Qoheleth resembling the former."[102] Also five grammatical features of Qumran literatures are compared with Qoheleth and concluded that "there is nothing unique to these texts and Qoheleth alone."[103]

Fredericks further takes the conclusions of Kropat and Polzin that differentiates the LBH features from EBH to show the commonality of Qoheleth with them. Under the same methodology which was used to compare the MH traits,[104] Fredericks enters to the section on evidence:[105] of the 12 categories, he lists 8 of them as equally EBH and LBH,[106] 2 as neither EBH nor LBH, 1 as more characteristic of EBH and 1 as Exclusively LBH. Among the nouns too, Fredericks find no

---

the grammatical categories in Copper scroll as well as in Bar-Koshiba letters resemble more closer to MH, where as Qoheleth firmly stands within the BH grammatical foundation. *Ibid.*, 117-119.

[102] *Ibid.*, 123.

[103] *Ibid.*, 123-124.

[104] Fredericks underlines his method under five categories: 1) Exclusively LBH, 2) Equally EBH and LBH, 3) More Characteristic of LBH: a. Independent of LBH, b. Dependent of LBH, 4) More Characteristic of EBH, 5) Neither EBH nor LBH. *Ibid.*, 125-129.

[105] He discusses the section on evidence under five grammatical parameters: verbs, nouns, pronouns, preposition and phonology.

[106] Eight Verbal Categories that are Equally EBH and LBH: the rarity of the *waw* consecutives imperfect are explained as the influence of genre (not historical narrative), the sole use of cohortative, infinitive construct with prepositional *lamed* in Qoheleth, infinitive construct with *beth* and *kaph* is too inconsistent in Biblical literature to point to dating, infinitive construct consecutive (only once in Qoheleth 9:1 and many times found in Biblical literature. Cf. Gen 42:25e, 1 Sam 8:12, Deu 26:17, etc), infinitive construct negated by *'ein* (3:14, cf. 1 Sam 9:7), infinitive absolute as a finite verb with conjunctive *waw* (8:9, 9:11. cf. Gen 41:43, Exo 8:11j, Jud 7:19, etc), participles as present tense, interchange of forms. *Ibid.*, 129-136.

exclusive case in favor of LBH.[107] The usages of pronouns do not favor the LBH proximity either.[108] Prepositions[109] and phonology[110] are also seen either as more characteristic of EBH or equally EBH and LBH. After comparing Qoheleth with LBH in 28 areas of grammar, this chapter concludes that there is nothing that convincingly proves the LBH connection in Qoheleth. Fredericks concludes that "in the light of this summary, an association of Qoheleth with LBH grammar is without support, rather the alignment is with EBH."[111]

Fredericks also takes on a detailed study of the vocabulary of Qoheleth. It is organized under these following five major sections: Mishnaisms, LBH Words, Aramaisms, Persianisms, and Greek words. Each section contains a methodological outline, evidence and summary sections. He carefully studies 36 words which are considered to be Mishnaisms and finds only four plausible cases. He points out that other EBH books also seems to have alleged Mishnaisms much more than

---

[107] The nouns ending in -*on* and -*uth* are attested, though not frequently, in EBH and taken as more characteristic of LBH, but independent of LBH. The singular-plural combination as well as consecutive *waw* patterns are closer to EBH, non-assimilated article (8:1, 6:10) is neither EBH nor LBH, nominative with *eth* is equally EBH. Ibid., 136-140.

[108] He discusses the 5 mostly used pronouns in Qoheleth – '*anî*, demonstrative feminine singular, relative pronoun subordinating an entire clause, relative pronoun (*sae*), pronoun with *eth*. *ani* is categorized as more characteristic of LBH but independent of LBH; *zoh* is taken as more characteristic of EBH (probably dialectical), and the other three are taken as equally EBH and LBH. Ibid., 141-150.

[109] Fredericks compares 6 prepositions to conclude that they are not characteristic of LBH: *beth* with relative pronoun, *lamed* as a sign of accusative, *lamed* with *ad*, *al* for directional *eal*, *al* in phrases denoting a state of being, compounded prepositions. Ibid., 150-154.

[110] *šae* for *še* is attributed to scribal error and it is equally EBH and LBH. Ibid., 155.

[111] Ibid., 159.

Qoheleth. The verdict is that the four cases do not offer adequate evidence to conclude strong Mishnaic influence upon Qoheleth. He also compares 23 supposed LBH words and finds only 3 closer to the claim. And so, its value is quite insignificant to place the book to a later period.[112] Fredericks analyses 48 alleged Aramaisms and narrows the list to 7. Out of this 4 has parallels in EBH sources or early Phoenician and 3 has parallels in later literature than EBH. 41 alleged Aramaisms are discounted due to reasons cited in the methodology. According to him, some Aramaic coloring is expected, as "Qoheleth has a wisdom / poetic / philosophic content and structure, criteria that would lead one to anticipate some Aramaisms."[113] The two Persian words are further explored as they are often cited as the evidence for the lateness of the language. After analyzing the two words, he observes that "Qoh has relatively few Persianisms and the two it has are acceptable for even a pre-exilic book given the historical connections of Palestine with the East."[114] He concludes "it is conceivable that the small degree to which Persianisms exist in Qoh does not demand a late date for the book's vocabulary."[115] He analyses six Hebrew phrases which are often cited as influenced by Greek language and thought. The conclusion is given as follows: "the supposed Greek influence on Qoh's vocabulary is unfounded. Alleged instances have adequate biblical precedent or natural Hebrew meanings and have no need for the explanation based on Greek."[116]

---

[112] Fredericks argues, "however, even the cumulative value of these is insignificant given the frequent situation in BH where a word surfaces only once or twice in EBH and then again in LBH. This is especially true when the grammatical nature of Qoh is void of any LBH influence." Ibid., 207.

[113] Ibid., 241.

[114] Ibid., 244.

[115] Ibid., 245.

[116] Ibid., 249.

Conclusions of Fredericks

The conclusion of Fredericks reminds the reader of the obvious importance given to the grammatical structure, over the lexical elements, while addressing language change. He points 17 colloquial elements in Qoheleth and leans towards North-Israelite influence. Fredericks offers few insightful concluding remarks in succinct narration: "the grammatical evidence therefore does not impose a date later than the exile, and would allow a pre-exilic time of composition. No significant cases of LBH or post-Biblical usage appeared in Qoheleth, and where there were similarities, other explanations were equally possible if not more probable that LBH or MH influences."[117] Lexical comparisons show that the apparent Aramaisms, Mishnaisms, Persianisms, etc are reduced under the methodology that was applied. And the first appearance of a word or the only occurrence of the word in Qoheleth and then in post-biblical books are not counted as evidences for lateness following the view of Barr, "naturally the adaptation of a word within Hebrew may have taken place a long time before the date of the earliest Hebrew text in which it appears."[118]

This summarizes the final position of Fredericks, "Qoheleth's language should not be dated any later than the exilic period, and no accumulation of linguistic evidence speaks against a pre-exilic date."[119] He also observes that "it is certain that Qoheleth does not find its closest similarities linguistically either in MH or in LBH. The peculiarities of the language find antecedents equally as often in EBH, if not more often than in LBH or MH."[120] The weakness of the consensus, according to

---

[117] *Ibid.*, 259.
[118] Barr, as quoted by Fredericks, *Ibid.*, 261.
[119] *Ibid.*, 262.
[120] *Ibid.*, 263.

him, was that they neglected the genre and dialectical uniqueness of Qoheleth. This neglect resulted in an ill-informed 'scholarly consensus of post-exilic date that is invalid.'[121] He finally remarks that the methodology of just listing the similarity between the LBH and MH is very doubtful as they do not take enough note of the earlier usages and their stylistic reasons. He encourages the serious reader to consider the cause for such usage and not to stop at the mere comparison of similarities.

Evaluation of Fredericks

Schoors makes the perceptive observation in his review of Fredericks that "this book will not go unnoted, for it totally upsets the modern critical approach to Qoheleth and particularly the *sensus communis* about its late post exilic date."[122] In fact, this book did get a lot of attention as it reignited the debate on the language of Qoheleth along with the conclusions of Isaksson. Fredericks treats every lexeme as well as grammatical traits and presents their precedence in Biblical Hebrew. Also, one of the notable characteristic of this book is its vast coverage of linguistic data and their bearing to the study of the language of Qoheleth. Fredericks compares the grammatical as well as lexical aspects of Qoheleth with MH, STH and LBH.[123] Such comparative approach has contributed a wealth of insights to the study of the language of Qoheleth.[124]

---

[121] *Ibid.*, 266.

[122] Antoon Schoors, "Review of Fredericks," *JBL* 108/4 (1989), 698.

[123] He goes into details when he deals with MH in which he differentiates the language of Tannaim (more of an oral dialect: used until 3rd AD) and of Amoraim (literary language, partially the revival of BH, used from 3rd – 5th AD).

[124] Schoors admiringly writes, "This is a careful study, based on research that has been carried out with great accuracy. It must be

Avi Hurvitz has been very critical towards Fredericks' approach.[125] In the words of Hurvitz, his review was mainly intended "to examine the principles and procedures underlying Fredericks' analysis."[126] After a rigorous evaluation of Fredericks' study, he contends that "Fredericks' answer cannot be considered definitive, since both the linguistic evidence adduced and its suggested interpretation is too often problematic and/or indecisive."[127] He argues along with the mainstream view, "in sum, the view that Qoheleth's language should be classified as classical/pre-exilic Hebrew is a challenging thesis, which seems recently to have gained some growing support in certain circles. It cannot be satisfactorily substantiated, however, on the basis of the philological analysis presented by Fredericks."[128]

---

recommended for its full attention to earlier uses, when it deals with features that at first sight could be MH or LBH...in general the argument is clear, thanks to the well organized structure of the book and explicit attention to the methodological side. It is also the most comprehensive study ever made on the subject." Schoors: Review of Fredericks, 699-700.

[125] Hurvitz formally appreciates the criticisms of various theories as well as his basic observation that Qoheleth is the only extant work of this kind which in itself demands certain linguistic singularity. Hurvitz titles this view as "nothing more than a working hypothesis." Avi Hurvitz, "Review of Fredericks," *Hebrew Studies* 31 (1990), 145.

[126] *Ibid.*, 152. Hurvitz lists four sample cases: 1)*'eyn* + *liqtol* as not having any chronological value is disputed (Cf, Deu. 4:2, 13:1); 2) Lexical comparison of יֹתֵר (root YTR – 2:15) is disputed that Qoheleth's adverbial usage is characteristic of MH/Aramaic and it cannot be described as *[e]qually (!) BH*; 3) The examples adduced from Ben Sira is not representative of its language in full compass; 4) *b^eken* as native to Israel (b+ken) is disputed. He prefers the conclusions of Schoors as sketched in "the pronouns of Qoheleth" and "the use of vowel letters in Qoheleth" that "the language of Qoheleth seems to belong to a later stage of development, one under Aramaic influence and already close to MH." *Ibid.*, 145-152.

[127] *Ibid.*, 145.

[128] *Ibid.*, 152.

Fredericks was criticized for being "too fanatical in his argumentation."[129] Fredericks' approach of pointing the lexical/grammatical precedence have resulted in a criticism that high concentration of late Hebrew features in itself "doesn't warrant an exclusively late identification, it may reveal a late predilection."[130] And Whybray supposes that the argument for affinity with EBH is the weakest in the book. It could be because of Whybray's preference for the Hellenistic background for Qoheleth. Whybray contends that 'to place Qoheleth in 8th – 7th BCE is to claim that he was a thinker several centuries ahead of his time.'[131] This conclusion of Whybray is betraying a personal affinity toward the later date. Snaith is more concerned about the fonts, typing errors and uneasy formatting of the book as such.[132] However, he points out that Fredericks had failed "to discuss how this genre of philosophical reflection fits in with such an early date."[133] However, he is appreciative of the study in general.

Though done independently, Fredericks' conclusions also point to the presence of a colloquial North Israelite dialect in Qoheleth; in that sense, it affirms the findings of Isaksson. Methodologically, in view of the materials covered, this is a monumental study that will continue to haunt critical

---

[129] Schoors: Review of Fredericks, 700.

[130] *Ibid.*, 700.

[131] However, Whybry does not go into the details of why he thinks that the argument is too weak. Norman Whybray, "Review of Fredericks," *The Expository Times 100* (1989-2000), 390. He also ends his review with a positive note that "his detailed analysis of Qoheleth's literary style contains much that will be of value for the serious student of the book." *Ibid.*, 390.

[132] Here Snaith wonders who should be blamed for: "are these defects the fault of the author or of printer's proofreaders?" John G. Snaith, "Review of Fredericks," *The Journal of Theological Studies* 41 (1990) 154.

[133] *Ibid.*, 155.

scholarship for years to come. In the words of Schoors, "the situation of those defending a post-exilic date of that language (as certainly most of us are) has become much more complicated."[134]

ANTOON SCHOORS, THE PREACHER SOUGHT TO FIND PLEASING WORDS, VOL. 1, 2 (1991 / 2004)

The books of Schoors were published when the post-exilic consensus for Qoheleth was under repeated questioning. Isaksson's study pointed that the verbal structures in Qoheleth remained distant from MH, and Fredericks argued the grammar as well as the vocabulary of the book is more in agreement with EBH than LBH and MH. These views, though a voice of minority scholarship, began to question the credibility of the general consensus. So, Schoors sets out to reassert the mainstream view that Qoheleth's language is late, and closely connected to LBH and MH, as well as to respond to the recent studies.

Schoors had written two volumes: the first volume deals extensively with the grammatical features and organized under three categories: Orthography and Phonetics, Morphology and Syntax. Its vocabulary is comprehensively dealt in the second volume. This division was necessitated, as Schoors notes, "in order not to delay the publication of our grammatical study."[135] In these two volumes, Schoors provides a reassessment of the recent studies as well as defends the consensus accepted by the mainstream scholarship.

Methodology

There is neither any implicit discussion nor any explicit outlining on methodology. However, the methodology Schoors

---

[134] Schoors: Review of Fredericks, 700.
[135] Schoors, *Pleasing words I*, 16.

adopts is obvious from the organization of his materials. From the two volumes and their progressive arguments, we come to understand that he adopts a lexical-grammatical analysis which primarily scrutinizes the grammatical aspect and examines the vocabularies and their individual lexemes. His organization reminds of the detailed outline of Siegfried who had done the earlier study in similar fashion, asserting the influence of LBH and MH on Qoheleth's language.[136]

Summary and Analysis

Schoors undertakes a meticulous study of the earlier scholarship in the introduction of his first volume. This survey legitimizes the need for his current monograph. Schoors calls the earlier work by Whitley as "disappointing as linguistic analysis"[137] and a partial reason behind his own study on the Qoheleth's language. [138] And more important reason for this study would be the work of Fredericks which Schoors considers as a serious threat to the LBH/MH influence consensus. And he undertakes this study not only to date the linguistic features but also to present a comprehensive description of the historical development of the Hebrew language, foreign influences, dialects and literary genre.[139]

---

[136] Seigfried's study (1898), closely following the work of Delitzsch (1875), provided a solid foundation for the LBH and MH influence on the language of Qoheleth. In fact, Schoors has bee appreciative of the systematic as well as exhaustive organization of Siegfried earlier. *Ibid.*, 2.

[137] This was the last linguistic study from the mainstream scholarship before Schoors. *Ibid.*, 13.

[138] He observes, "it was my partial dissatisfaction with this work which brought me to organize my own research in the format of a grammar and a vocabulary." *Ibid.*, 13.

[139] *Ibid.*, 16.

At first, he focuses on the orthography and phonetics: The interchange between *sin* and *samekh*[140] and *bᵉ* and *p*.[141] He cites seven late examples and draws the conclusion that "in this respect, Qoheleth's orthography seems to be late."[142] The orthography of vowels focuses on the defective and plene orthography in Qoheleth.[143] It was earlier argued by Dahood that the use of vowel letters were due to the Phoenician influence.[144] But Schoors takes most of Dahood's examples as textual variants. He points out that "Qoheleth represents a somewhat middle stage in the development of plene writing [in the chronology of Hebrew language]."[145] The orthography related to Kethibh - Qere is dealt in the ensuing discussion and the superiority of Qere is upheld as has been done traditionally.[146] In the section on the phonetics of the consonants, Schoors observes three weak consonants: *aleph*, *he* and *yod*. He examines two cases of the elision of *aleph* (4:14, 12:5 – scribal error) and the unusual positioning of *aleph* in 11:3

---

[140] 1:17 uses *sin*, whereas 2:3, 12, 13, 7:25, 10:1, 13 employs *samekh*.

[141] The issue is connected to *p'l* in 8:8 which was taken by Dahood as an equivalent of *b'l* "to make / to work" in Ugaritic. But Schoors disputes this connection and offers an alternative reading. *Ibid.*, 21-22.

[142] *Ibid.*, 20.

[143] This section is a complete incorporation of Schoors' 1988 article in *Ugarit Forschungen*. See, Antoon Schoors, "The Use of Vowel Letters in Qoheleth," *UF* 20 (1988): 277-286.

[144] See, M. Dahood, "Canaanite-Phoenician Influence in Qoheleth," *Biblica* 33 (1952), 43.

[145] He summarizes his observation, "in sum, in a total of 242 instances, where internal *scriptio plena* was possible, only 127 have it, whereas 115 have a defective writing." *Ibid.*, 32.

[146] Schoors follow the trails of Jouon and Gordis in his study of Kethibh – Qere. However, Schoors sees that largely Kethib-Qere variants doesn't affect the meaning of the text. And mostly he prefers the Qere with few exceptions. *Ibid.*, 40.

יְהוּא is explained as a late form.¹⁴⁷ Schoors breaks down the topic on *he* with the elision of article and *hiphil*: Though there are many unpredictable usage of definite article in the later books, such traits are also attested in the early books;¹⁴⁸ the omission of *he* in *hiphil* preformative is taken as a late trait. He also points out the phonetic change form *yi* to *'i* in the later period.¹⁴⁹ Issues related to the phonetics of the vowels (*a>â* and *â>û*) is taken as the Masoretic preference on vocalization and something that was present in LXX.¹⁵⁰

He further explores the morphology of Qoheleth, which is categorized under five major sections: pronoun,¹⁵¹ the noun, numerals, the verb and particles. Schoors deals with five kinds of pronouns: personal pronoun, demonstrative pronoun, relative pronoun, interrogative pronoun and indefinite pronoun. He sees the frequency of *'anî* and the absence of *anôchî* as the pointer to the latter date.¹⁵² The demonstrative pronoun (זֶה/זוֹ) is taken as pointing to "the linguistic development which is already close to the Mishnaic one."¹⁵³ The 32 occurrences of זֹה, זֶה without article is explained as the result of being used

---

¹⁴⁷ Schoors observes that "in MH, this form often has the same non-jussive force as the hypothetical יְהוּא." *Ibid.*, 40-43.

¹⁴⁸ Here, Schoors engages the word from 8:1. *Ibid.*, 44.

¹⁴⁹ *Ibid.*, 44-45.

¹⁵⁰ *Ibid.*, 45-46.

¹⁵¹ Antoon Schoors, "The Pronouns in Qoheleth." *HS* 30 (1989): 71-90.

¹⁵² Here, Schoors sees a very strong evidence for the later date. He discredits the views of Isakson (Northern Hebrew dialect) and Fredericks (vernacular element) and concludes "it needs some special pleading to maintain that this distribution has no chronological significance." *Ibid.*, 48.

¹⁵³ He rules out the suggestion of Fredericks (this form as dialectal uniqueness) as without proof. *Ibid.*, 53.

substantivally, not as an adjective.¹⁵⁴ He lists the usage of the relative pronoun *še* as 'belonging to the later phase of the language, standing midway between BH and MH.'¹⁵⁵ He finds Qoheleth's usage of interrogative and indefinite pronoun as akin to Mishna.¹⁵⁶

The following section on the noun is further divided into the formation of nouns, gender, number, case-endings, noun with suffix, and inflectional irregularities. Noun formations are taken as closer to Mishna.¹⁵⁷ Under the section on gender, he studies the feminine nouns ending with *–t* and shows similar biblical examples appear in the late literatures.¹⁵⁸ The small section on gender substitution in Qoheleth accepts with Fredericks that it is not a convincing trait of MH.¹⁵⁹ As far the number is concerned, he finds duals in Qoheleth as generally pointing to the later stage of Hebrew language.¹⁶⁰ He also sees the usage of the number 100 as a feature very frequently attested in Mishna and Talmud, though there are biblical precedence (cf. Gen 26:12, 2 Sam 24:3, Prov 17:10).¹⁶¹ In the section on the

---

¹⁵⁴ It was taken by Dahood as the Phoenician influence upon Qoheleth. But Schoors observes, as a pronoun in substantival position, it never takes article in BH. *Ibid.*, 54.

¹⁵⁵ Schoors' conclusion on this is "either it belongs to the northern Hebrew or it's of late." *Ibid.*, 56.

¹⁵⁶ *Ibid.*, 57-60.

¹⁵⁷ Here Schoors studies various noun types such as *Qatâl*, *Qᵉtîl*, *Qᵉtîlâ*, *Qalqal*, forms with prefixed *mem*, *Qitlôn/qitlân*, nouns ending with *–ût*, nouns ending with *–ôt*. He repeatedly comes to the conclusion that the forms are much closer to the nouns used in the post biblical Hebrew. *Ibid.*, 60-67.

¹⁵⁸ The word he studies is מִקְלָשַׁחַת (8:8). *Ibid.*, 67-68.

¹⁵⁹ *Ibid.*, 69.

¹⁶⁰ *Ibid.*, 72.

¹⁶¹ The usage of the numeral 100 is also attested in Ugaritic. *Ibid.*, 75-76.

morphology of verbs, he denies the presence of *Yiphil* (1.18) as claimed by Dahood and takes it as 'an imperfect of proverbial sayings.'[162] The rarity of imperfect consecutives is taken as the affinity of the language with the later biblical books and of the Mishna.[163] Schoors agrees with Fox who takes 9:14-15 as a piece of narrative which employs a morpheme much different from the classical grammar. Adverbs are studied then as demonstrative adverbs, asseverative adverbs, nouns with adverbial function, temporal adverbs, and enclitic *mem*, and deals with number of morphemes. His observations on the prepositions led him to prefer the late date explanations than accepting any other influence of Phoenician.[164] Among the conjunctions used in Qoheleth, he finds few cases which were used increasingly in the Late Hebrew.[165] He takes the interjection אִי in 10:16 and cites its prevalence in the MH and Jewish Aramaic and concludes, "in any case, the interjection אִי is definitely late.[166]

He also expounds on the syntax under three major divisions: the clause and its parts, syntax of clauses and syntactic and stylistic varia. The subdivision on "the clause and its parts" covers number of syntactical elements. Schoors take the frequent use of אִין in the nominal class as characteristic of

---

[162] *Ibid.*, 79.

[163] *Ibid.*, 86.

[164] *Ibid.*, 121-124.

[165] אִלּוּ occurs twice in the Old Testament (Eccl. 6:6, Est 7:4). Though it was rare in Bible, it was widely used in the MH as well as Jewish Aramaic and Syriac, with the exception of Qumran. So Schoors take it definitely pointing to the late composition. *Ibid.*, 136. The use of *asher* instead of *ki* is observed by Schoors, though appears in the early biblical books, increasingly used in the late biblical books. *Ibid.*, 144. Also the composite conjunctions with *še/asher* also as pointers of much later usage. *Ibid.*, 144-148.

[166] *Ibid.*, 149.

BH, contrary to Whitley.[167] Also Qoheleth's use of pronominal nouns as copula also has BH attestation, contrary to Dahood.[168] Generally, he thinks that the nominal clause in Qoheleth is well within the BH grammar with occasional traits of lateness.[169] The section on the verbal clause briefly deals with the issue of subject and how the general subjects are expressed either in 3rd person singular or plural.[170] Also frequent lack of concord in Qoheleth is attributed to the colloquial language.[171] With regard to the word order, object comes early in the sentences. Schoors remarks, "this stylistic peculiarity is certainly connected with Qoh's argumentative style, which continually calls for emphasis and contrast."[172] The syntax of the personal pronouns explicates various syntactical functions personal pronouns in Qoheleth. Schoors argues that Qoheleth's use of *hem* instead of *hen* as pointer to "represent a late stage of Hebrew" and rejects the proposal of Dahood that this feature is induced by the Phoenician influence on the syntax (2:6, 10, 10:9, 11:8, 12:1).[173] The use of article in the syntax is discussed in connection with the views of Dahood and Delsman. However, Schoors observes that "we find that in other Biblical books the use of the article is not so consistent."[174] And he

---

[167] Whitley takes the usage of אין with the pronominal suffix is characteristic of MH. *Ibid.*, 152.

[168] Dahood evokes a 5th century Inscription of Yehawmilk to argue for the Phoenician influence. *Ibid.*, 153.

[169] He agrees with Delsman that verses like 3.18 and 9:4 would be totally impossible in classical Hebrew. *Ibid.*, 153.

[170] As Qoheleth makes number of general observations, such usage became quite prevalent. *Ibid.*, 154-157.

[171] Ginsburg argued that in a colloquial language, people are not always particular about making a verb agree with its subject. Schoors follows this lead. *Ibid.*, 158-159.

[172] *Ibid.*, 160.

[173] *Ibid.*, 163.

[174] *Ibid.*, 169.

concludes, "in sum, Qoh's irregular use of the article has classical antecedents but the higher frequency of it could betray a later stage of the language, close to MH."[175] As to the syntax of the verb, generally Qoheleth uses perfect tense to refer to past activities and situations, and sometimes perfect is also used to refer present events (cf. 3:15).[176] In Qoheleth, there are also large numbers of imperfect verbs which express habitual ideas.[177] Qoheleth also uses many infinitive absolutes which was observed by Dahood to be "[of] Pheonician syntactical influence rather than to the mere lateness of the language."[178] In fact, this is the only case Schoors considers to be a strong case in favor of Dahood. And he also mentions that the frequent employment of infinitive absolute as finite verbs in the later books should be taken as alternative explanation.[179] Usually the frequent uses of participles as frequentatives / present tense are thought to be due to the Qoheleth's late use of language.[180] Here, Schoors does not present his position, but implicitly prefers the mainstream consensus. Accusatives are treated in detail in the next category: Schoors particularly thinks that "את with subject" (אֶת־הָאִשָּׁה) is used more in the later texts and frequent in Mishna.[181] In the following section, "syntax of prepositions," Schoors explores the various prepositions used in Qoheleth. The discussion on preposition ב is lengthy as Schoors tackles with the proposals of Dahood, who terms the use of prepositions in Qoheleth as "an unhebraic," and rejects

---

[175] Ibid., 170f.

[176] Here Schoors follows the lead of Isaksson with slight updating. Ibid., 172-175.

[177] Such traits are common for wisdom genre. Ibid., 175-177.

[178] Dahood, Biblica 33 (1952), 49-50.

[179] Schoors, Pleasing Words I, 180

[180] Many scholars come to this conclusion, including Whitley, Fox, Lauha, Delsman, Aalders and Segal. Ibid., 184.

[181] He is supported by Gordis and Segal. Ibid., 191-192.

them.[182] The use of the preposition is accepted עַל as "a late phenomenon influenced by Aramaic, in line with the majority of the scholars."[183]

"The syntax of clauses" analyzes the grammar of seven different kinds of clauses used in Qoheleth. Co-ordinate clauses explain the various usages of *waw* by Qoheleth as he delicately contrasts the traditional wisdom of proverbs.[184] Interrogative clauses discuss the rhetorical questions which Qoheleth frequently uses to express his observations emphatically.[185] Schoors also identifies circumstantial clause along with Delitzsch in 2:3 and 12:13.[186] A brief section deals with the subject clauses with one example from 4:17. While discussing object clauses, he supposes the usage of ה... אוֹ (2:16, 11:6) is quiet common in direct disjunctive questions in MH. He prefers a late feature conclusion here, but delays it as the evidences at hand are rather scanty.[187] The section on the relative clause is further divided into three: asyndetic relative clause, retrospective pronoun or suffix, varia. Schoors sees the omission of the pronominal suffix referring back to the antecedent of a relative clause, though known in other biblical books, is similar to the one of MH.[188] He observes that Qoheleth uses nominal

---

[182] *Ibid.*, 193-199.

[183] Schoors rejects the explanation of Dahood that לְ and עַל have often same meaning in Punic, and that it could be used interchangeably. *Ibid.*, 200.

[184] *Ibid.*, 204-206.

[185] *Ibid.*, 206f.

[186] However, he is quiet doubtful of reading the second instance as a circumstantial clause. He prefers to take it as a main clause or as an exhortation as it doesn't have the *waw* in the beginning of the sentence. *Ibid.*, 208f.

[187] *Ibid.*, 209.

[188] *Ibid.*, 212f.

RECENT STUDIES ON THE LANGUAGE OF QOHELETH   61

particles such as אִם, אִלּוּ, כַּאֲשֶׁר to introduce conditional clauses. He simply cites the observations of Delitzsch that there are asyndetic conditional clauses in Qoheleth with slight variations.[189]

Further, Schoors expounds five specific syntactic and stylistic varias. The stylistic feature known as Anticipation is inserting the part of the sentence earlier than its logical place, it is frequently used in Qoheleth (2:24, 3:13, 21, 4:4, 5:18, 6:10, 9:11, 10:3, 11:8). Qoheleth's use of hendiadys[190] is briefly discussed here from various authors' points of view. Merism, expressions of totality, are listed out (3:11 מֵרֹאשׁ וְעַד־סוֹף "from beginning to the end," 10:13 תְּחִלַּת...וְאַחֲרִית "at the beginning... at the end," 9:10 מַעֲשֶׂה וְחֶשְׁבּוֹן וְדַעַת וְחָכְמָה "all human activity," 6:2 עֹשֶׁר וּנְכָסִים וְכָבוֹד "everything man can desire," 11:6 בַּבֹּקֶר...וְלָעֶרֶב "at all times," 10:6 נִתַּן...יֵשְׁבוּ – example of Merism in verbal construction). Numerical gradation in Qoheleth (4:12, 11:9), Schoors argues following Whitley, are within the parameter of Biblical wisdom tradition, that any attribution to Canaanite influence is unwarranted.[191]

The second volume of Schoors focuses on the vocabularies in Qoheleth. Schoors outlines the intention of this study as "for each lexeme that occurs in Qoh, I study the use of that lexeme

---

[189] Delitzsch treats 5:13 as asyndetic conditional clause. But Schoors takes it as conditional protasis. *Ibid.*, 213.

[190] Two words connected by a conjunction to express a compound/ complex idea is known as Hendiadys. It literally means "one through two" (Gk. *hen-dia-duoin*).

[191] Biblical wisdom tradition gives enough examples of numerical gradation: two-three (Isa 17:6, Sir 23:16), three-four (Am 1-2, Prov 30:15,18,21,29, Sir 26:5), Six-seven (Job 5:19, Prov 6:16), Seven-eight (Micah 5:4), nine-ten (Sir 25:7). *Ibid.*, 219.

in all its contexts in this biblical book."[192] He studies 29 vocabularies in the first chapter, mainly focusing on their frequency, semantic meaning in other parts of the Old Testament and their unique usage in Qoheleth. The second chapter, titled as "words less frequently used yet typical of Qoheleth," explicates 31 words occasionally emphasizing the lateness of the semantic usage.[193] As part of the third chapter, a huge volume of 161 words are studied under the title "classical BH words less or not typical of Qoheleth." Chapter 4, studies 40 words which occur only in Qoheleth. Schoors points out the absence of other reference to most of these words in biblical corpus and adduces examples from MH and QH to explain their lateness.[194] The final chapter, titled "words which requires no special analysis," studies 187 words, its meaning and number of occurrences within Qoheleth, probably they didn't invoke much scholarly contention.

Conclusions of Schoors

Schoors gives an interim conclusion at the end of the first volume. The conclusion is given under five points. He also projects to reaffirm them at the end of his lexical study in the second volume. First conclusion recognizes the difficulty of reaching a firm conclusion when there is such a diversity of details and he agrees with Isaksson that the verbs conform with the classical usage to large extent. Second conclusion firmly asserts that "the language of Qoheleth is definitely late in the

---

[192] Generally, he explains the frequency of the lexical occurrence in the OT and in Qoheleth. Then he moves on to interact with the scholarly works to define the meaning of each words in its context. Schoors, *Pleasing Words II*, 1.

[193] While studying the word *salit*, Schoors cites the conclusion of Wagner (1966) to defend the case put forward by Fredericks (1988) without any further discussion. *Ibid.*, 246f.

[194] See, *Ibid.*, 427-432, 444, 447, 466, 468, 470.

development of BH and belongs to what Scholars have recently called Late Biblical Hebrew (LBH)... this conclusion confirms the general consensus among critical scholars."[195] Third conclusion rejects the Aramaic translation theory but accepts that there are some Aramaic features in the book, which Schoors take as "later traits."[196] The fourth conclusion concerns Dahood's Phoenician theory and Schoors concludes that "out of some 30 linguistic phenomena which Dahood has invoked in favor of his theory, barely one could more or less stand the test."[197] The fifth conclusion is related to the bearings of genre and the presence of a dialect in the book. While pondering such possibility, Schoors observes, "a general distribution of a large number of features taken together shows them to be late at the same time." From the conclusions of the first volume, it is clear that Schoors has chosen to date the book late based on the study of grammar.

The conclusions of the second volume are, in his opinion, affirming what he stated in his first volume.[198] There are four conclusions listed here: first conclusion recognizes that the vocabulary exhibits the "highly reflective and even philosophical character of the Book of Qoheleth."[199] The second conclusion points that about 30 lexemes in Qoheleth are characteristic of LBH and that it should be classified as late book.[200] The third conclusion points out that there are many

---

[195] Schoors, *Pleasing Words I*, 222-223.

[196] *Ibid.*, 223.

[197] *Ibid.*, 223.

[198] Schoors notes, "...this vocabulary confirms the interim conclusion of vol. 1 about the late date of the language." Schoors, *Pleasing Words II*, 499.

[199] *Ibid.*, 499.

[200] Schoors observes, "the lexical study of this book shows again that the language of Qoh is definitely late in the development of BH and belong to LBH." *Ibid.*, 499.

lexical Aramaisms. He agrees with the Aramaic influence on Qoheleth's language and takes it to point to the later date.[201] In the fourth conclusion (misprinted as No.3), he observes, "there are no compelling arguments to accept an important Greek influence in Qoheleth's vocabulary."[202] Though he is unsure of the Greek influence in Qoheleth's vocabulary, he allows such plausibility in its content. Schoors fifth conclusion confronts Seow's study which argues for the Persian period dating for Qoheleth. Schoors agrees with the *terminus ante quam* proposed by Seow but differs in his dating to the Persian period. The main argument of Seow that Qoheleth's use of economic vocabularies points to the commercial environment of Persian period is negated by Schoors, where he argues that the terms might have had economic meaning, "but in Qoh the latter indisputably has a broader sapiental meaning..."[203]

Evaluation of Schoors

Schoors has given a thorough survey of the language of Qoheleth in a systematic and elegantly organized manner than any of his predecessors. First volume is very valuable to trace the history of scholarship on the language of Qoheleth. His survey is wide-ranging and interacts adequately with works published in Hebrew, along with the works from English and German.[204] Schoors is taking side with the general scholarly

---

[201] There is a misprint. Instead of conclusion No.3, No.2 is misprinted two times. I'll follow the corrected style. *Ibid.*, 500.

[202] But he feels that there are some parallels available in the domain of content, rather than language. He hints that it might be available in his forthcoming commentary. *Ibid.*, 501.

[203] He further states, "I hold the conviction that it is easier to situate Qoh's language in the Hellenistic than in the Persian Period." *Ibid.*, 502.

[204] In fact, He is the only author who mentions about Eleyonai's contribution in his bibliography. And references to whose works are generally absent in English scholarship.

consensus. The organization of his work definitely recalls the earlier work by Seigfried. Clemens admiringly observes, "This systematic treatment makes the book a very useful reference work, providing ready access to every debatable linguistic form through the comprehensive table of contents and extensive reference index."[205] This contribution of presenting the update on the studies on Qoheleth's language is commendable.

However, Schoors was criticized for several of his positions. He does not provide any methodological statements in neither of his books. Clemens observes that, "he [Schoors] perpetuates previous scholarship in appearing to count rather than to weigh evidence"[206] and also notices "the tendency to enumerate rather than evaluate."[207] Since the procedure employed is flawed, the conclusion it leads to is also under question. Also, rather than interacting with the latest scholarly questions, he has very laboriously and indefinitely argued against the 'already discredited and outdated' Phoenician Influence theory of Dahood in the first volume.[208]

Seven aspects of Schoors' conclusions are criticized by Clemens: 1) Schoors take the substitution of the sibilants in Qoheleth as pointer to late tendency. However, Clemens argues that it is liable to dialectal interference and so not significant

---

[205] D. M. Clemens, "Review of Schoors," *JNES* 56/2 (1997), 151.

[206] "If a linguistic feature has eight late attested parallels and one early, it tends to become an evidence for lateness. While this may be valid (or the best that can be done at this stage), it is nevertheless simplistic in view of the relatively scanty preservation of materials from the biblical period and of information concerning their origins." Ibid., 151.

[207] Ibid., 151.

[208] It is respectable to recognize that Schoors does not agree with Dahood's theory. But is it necessary to deal with Dahood's theory in such extensive manner, since it was already discredited decades ago? May be, it is the way of paying tributes to his mentor M. J. Dahood.

chronologically. 2) Schoors takes the orthography of Qoheleth to point to later date. Hurvitz also attests to the view of Schoors on orthography.[209] But Clemens along with Barr takes it that "orthography is still inadequate as an index by which to date the language or origins of a composition."[210] 3) The noun forms that end in –*ut* and their lateness are questioned.[211] 4) The exclusive use of *'anî* as a identifier for lateness is rejected.[212] 5) The conclusion that *zôh* is late and of Northern origin is also questioned.[213] 6) The frequency of the relative particle *še* implies a late date / northern origin is disputed.[214] 7) Qoheleth's non-use of Imperfect Consecutive is traditionally understood as evidence for the late date. This conclusion is also questioned.[215]

---

[209] Hurvitz: Review of Fredericks, 152.

[210] James Barr has pointed out the difficulty of the orthographic dating of any biblical writing: 1) Masoretic orthography is consistently inconsistent, 2) there is no discernible system, in contrast to the position of Cross and Freedman, followed by Schoors; 3) there is no possibility of dating the texts from their orthography, and probably none of them reflects original spelling; 4) while there is a tendency for earlier or later texts to be more defective or plene, respectively, there are frequent exceptions to this pattern. Clemens: Review of Schoors, 152-153.

[211] Fredericks argues that the reason why Qoheleth uses such nouns could be for literary reasons. Also, there are pre-exilic examples available. Fredericks, *Qoheleth's language*, 137-138. Also, if the morpheme –*at* is ancient, it could have been used in any period and has very limited chronological significance.

[212] Clemens notes that "it is difficult, though, to substantiate the predominance of *'nky* at any well-defined period; and *'ny* prevails in pre-exilic texts also." See, Clemens: Review of Schoors, 153.

[213] There are pre-exilic examples of same form (Jud 18:4, 2 Sam 11:25). It is unattested in Qumran and other pre-Mishnaic texts. It could be an archaic form survived into late Hebrew. *Ibid.*, 153.

[214] *Še* occurs more in late texts is not an established conclusion, there are seven early examples. *Ibid.*, 153.

[215] In the prophetic literature, when they talk about future or general truth, CsI is sparingly used. (Cf. Zephaniah, Zachariah 9-14). This is also attributed to the semi-narrative style of Qoheleth.

Second volume dwarfs the first one in size which is well over 500 pages. The book itself has generally drawn appreciation.[216] However, most of the reviewers have expressed some sense of arbitrariness in the organization of the lexemes as it is obviously subjective and does not seem to have been divided based on any sound methodology.[217] In fact, it is indisputably a hard challenge to classify all the vocabularies of Qoheleth.

If the introduction of Part I was its strength, Part II stands on the other extreme. Schoors gets directly to the study of the vocabularies with the briefest one page introduction for a gigantic 500 pages book. Again the issue of methodology is pointed out here by Rogland, "As a whole, however, the study suffers greatly from having very ill-defined parameters. One is never exactly sure what particular questions the author is attempting to answer here: is it in fact intended as a lexicographical study?"[218] The study for sure lacks a sense of direction and without over-arching structure that provides cohesiveness.

---

[216] Rogland positively comments, "there is undeniably a great deal of erudition displayed throughout the work in the analysis of the textual data, and the wealth of exegetical and bibliographical resources gathered here would be useful to anyone interested in the interpretation of Qoheleth." Max Rogland, "Review of Schoors II," *RBL* (2006), 2.

[217] Rogland observes, "There is a good deal of subjectivity inherent in such a mode of organization." *Ibid.*, 2. Vogels gently notes that, "the method of classification chosen by Schoors is not always obvious." W. F. Walter Vogels, "Review of Schoors II," *Theoforum 37* (2006), 85. Miller also perceives similar issue, "these titles appear to be handy working categories for Schoors' research, but are imprecise and somewhat arbitrary for those hoping to use the book as a reference tool." Douglas B. Miller, "Review of Schoors II," *Biblica 88/2* (2007), 260.

[218] Rogland: Review of Schoors II, 2.

Rogland is admittedly negative in his assessment of this book. He sees Schoors drawing unnecessary conclusions in the first and second chapters. While explicating the word היה and its translation in Qoheleth as "happen," Schoors comes to the conclusion that Qoheleth "is a real philosopher but more interested in human life than in an ontology of an unalterable metaphysical world" obviously stepping beyond the study of lexicography into theological discussion.[219] Also, he does the same with the study of the word הָאֱלֹהִים.[220] The major treatment of *hebel* and its translation as "absurd" gives one the insight into the direction Schoors moves. Miller strongly objects the translation of *hebel* as "absurd" and favors the symbolic translation "vapor."[221]

Another 'Achilles Heel' of this book is that, in spite of the volume of bibliographical information, it misses some of the seminal studies pertaining to the language of Qoheleth. Even though, the book of Young was released in 1993, there is no interaction with Young's approach. Also references to important works like Barr and Silva are also missing. It might lead one to wonder, whether it is unintentional or the author is purposely leaving out certain works that would significantly destabilize his position. And the absence of direct preference to Hellenistic dating, except only a passing hint, is also criticized.[222] Rogland

---

[219] While such conclusion makes one wonder the focus of the study itself, also such conclusions cannot be decided by the study of a single lexeme. It is too narrow to come to such broad conclusions.

[220] Again, Rogland is very perceptive as he notes that "it is a linguistic fallacy to attribute this much contextual information to any single lexeme in an utterance." *Ibid.*, 3.

[221] See, Douglas. B. Miller, "Qoheleth's Symbolic Use of הבל," *JBL* 117/3 (1998): 437-454.

[222] Rogland satirically writes, "I think the reader is justified in feeling rather shortchanged at this point: Where else ought one to make a case

ably summarizes his conclusions about the breadth of the usefulness of this book as follows:

> "One must therefore use this book with a great deal of caution as a source of linguistic information. While it will be useful for the exegetical scholar, the results for the linguist or the lexicographer will be rather disappointing. Although organized somewhat differently, the work is very much akin to the standard theological dictionaries of Kittel and the like, which, though informative in their own way, are severely limited in usefulness from a linguistic standpoint."[223]

IAN YOUNG, DIVERSITY IN PRE-EXILIC HEBREW, 1993

Ian Young, Associate Professor in the Department of Semitic Studies at the University of Sydney,[224] entered the debate of the dating of Biblical books with his unconventional book titled, "Diversity in Pre-Exilic Hebrew."[225] This is a break-through study that has criticized the methodology of the standard linguistic dating of biblical works from a distinctive vantage point. While taking into account the linguistic fluctuations within the biblical corpus, Young does not seek the chronological development from within the text alone. Rather, he brings in the entire linguistic milieu, in which Hebrew as a language came into existence and flourished, to bear upon the much debated question of Qoheleth's language. This fresh

---

for the date of Qoheleth's language, if not after a five-hundred-page study of the book's vocabulary, which itself follows an over two-hundred-page study of its grammar? In the end, one gets the feeling that one has been 'chasing the wind' all along, which is indeed a vexation and a grievous evil under the sun!" Rogland: Review of Schoors II, 3-4.

[223] *Ibid.*, 3.

[224] Ian Young: *http://www.arts.usyd.edu.au/departs/hbjs/staff/profiles/young.shtml* (Accessed on August 24, 2009).

[225] Ian Young, *Diversity in Pre-Exilic Hebrew* (Tubingen: J.C.B. Mohr, 1993).

approach has garnered much praise and also criticisms from various scholarly quarters.[226]

Young takes the wider spectrum of Hebrew language in sight, as he assesses the current views in the scholarly world with regard to chronological dating. His conclusions on the development of the Hebrew language also bear upon the so-called late books which show the 'signs of LBH characteristics' like Aramaizing, Mishnaizing, appearance of loanwords, etc. He observes, "Pre-exilic Hebrew is conceived as being a rather monolithic entity often called Standard Biblical Hebrew (SBH)… the assumption that this Standard Biblical Hebrew was the Hebrew of pre-exilic times allows other non-standard works to be judged."[227] He also questions the current predominant categorization of Qoheleth as late book:

> "Qoheleth is Aramaizing, Mishnaizing, and also seems to contain Persian loanwords. It does not fit in with the monolithic Standard Biblical corpus, so therefore it must be Late Biblical Hebrew. Yet the internal evidences of the book, especially the advice about conduct in the Royal Court, would place Qoheleth self-evidently in the monarchic period. It is obvious in such a case that the orthodox understanding of Biblical Hebrew is inadequate to comprehend the language of Qoheleth."[228]

---

[226] An online buyer/reviewer praised Young for his fresh approach to the issue of dating: "Mr. Young's analysis of biblical Hebrew is one of a rare examples of Old Testament scholarship showing awareness of how language really works. In contrast to many other approaches in this field which have not been able to free themselves of a somewhat naive and simplifying classroom smell, this book is in tune with the methodological standards of modern linguistic fieldwork." Review of Diversity in Pre-Exilic Hebrew, *http://www.amazon.com/Diversity-Pre-Exilic-Hebrew-Forschungen-Testament/product-reviews/3161460588/ ref=cm_cr_dp_all_helpful?ie=UTF8&coliid=&showViewpoints=1&colid=&sortBy= bySubmissionDateDescending* (Accessed on October 2, 2009).

[227] Young, *Diversity*, 1.

[228] *Ibid.*, 2.

Young interacts with various areas of scholarly contention pertinent to the book of Qoheleth (140-157) to suggest the dating of the book, of which the section on the language is more relevant to this research.

Methodology

This book opts for non-chronological methodology, which incorporates the presently available knowledge on Hebrew Language. It seeks to enhance the current procedure of dating, especially the difficult texts, by going beyond mere lexical comparisons and adducing epigraphical references as definite factors for determining chronological conclusions. This approach is explicated well in the introduction, "the aim of this book is to suggest a new model for the Hebrew of the Biblical Period, one which is better able to comprehend the evidence... what is new, we believe, is the consistency with which the new picture is applied to explain all the evidence."[229]

Summary and Analysis

Young begins by theorizing the pre-existence of Hebrew as prestige language of diverse Canaan and the adaptation of this language by the ethnically and linguistically diverse constituents of the people of Israel. Two important conclusions emerge out of this study: there was a large and varied number of possible influences on the language of Israelites in the early period, which includes Indo-Aryan, Hurrian, Philistine and other languages;[230] and Biblical Hebrew as the continuation of the pre-literary language of Syria Palestine.[231] He moves on to

---

[229] Young, *Diversity*, 2.

[230] The very argument of diversity at the formation of Hebrew makes the theory that holds foreign loanwords as pointer to late influence, quite shaky.

[231] Young, *Diversity*, 11.

study Hebrew in the context of other Northwest Semitic languages which includes Phoenician, Moabite, Edomite, Ammonite, the Deir Alla Dialect, Aramaic, and the Philistians. Most important is the section on the criteria for underlining the date for the loanwords. Here, Young points out "their relative uselessness as chronological markers,"[232] as much of the current studies dwell in the realm of hypotheses and insufficient data to draw their conclusions. The chronology of Hebrew language and its various phases of development, i.e., Archaic, Standard, Late and Mishnaic Hebrew are studied in depth in the third chapter. He advocates a fresh approach towards the inscriptions that comes from pre-exilic period and also analyses the differences between the official Hebrew employed in the inscriptions with the standard language used in the writing of the Biblical corpus.

Chapter five is of extreme importance to this research, as it discusses the linguistic diversity in the pre-exilic language and its bearing on understanding and dating Qoheleth. He treats other themes too before focusing on the language. He observes the consensus and states that, "it is on the basis of the language, and to a lesser degree, the thought of the book, that Qoheleth is dated, usually to the Hellenistic period."[233] Young undertakes a survey of the proposed late thought in Qoheleth, in which he tackles issues such as Hellenistic influence, life after

---

[232] He sets three criteria for using loanwords in dating: 1) The foreign word must have a firmly established origin and foreign etymology; 2) We should be able to give a plausible reason for the travel of a word at a certain point and explain also why this is not possible in an earlier period; 3) We should be able to demonstrate that the particular loan has a function only in the late works, or works known to have been composed after the probable date of borrowing. Young goes on to suggest that "we need more solid criteria for defining chronological strata of Biblical Hebrew than can be found in the speculative field of loanwords." Young, *Diversity*, 72.

[233] Young, *Diversity*, 140.

death, near eastern background, the integrity of Qoheleth, etc. Regarding the Hellenistic influence, he affirms with Barton that Qoheleth is not dependent on Greek influences but its foundations are firmly set within Hebrew wisdom tradition.[234] He holds that themes like criticism of God and orthodox religion are also found in books like Job (Job 7:16b-18). So, he concludes that "there is no need, therefore, to postulate the breakdown of traditional beliefs under the impact of Hellenism as the occasion for the thought of Qoheleth. Qoheleth could have written the same things at any time in Israelite history."[235] Also, he views Qoheleth, not only as a reaction to the wisdom tradition of Israel, but against the dominant belief in covenant theology.[236] He also sees the difficulty of dating based on the perceived historical allusions in the books which are inconclusive. He provides a strong case for a pre-exilic date as he compares Qoheleth's teachings about the court procedure and etiquette, the teaching which is almost absent from Ben Sira.[237] He remarks that "the fact that there is king and royal court near at hand is presupposed throughout the book… the

---

[234] Barton argues that "the book of Ecclesiastes represents, then, an original development of Hebrew thought, thoroughly Semitic in its point of view, and quiet independent of Greek influences." Barton, *Ecclesiastes*, 43.

[235] Some of the symbols that correspond to afterlife and resurrection are lotus chains, the cherubim. See, John Strange, "Theology and Politics in Architecture and Iconography," *SJOT* 5/1 (1991): 23-44. Young points out that "…his (Qoheleth's) mention of them (concept of life after death) would not disqualify even the idea of Solomonic authorship" as Solomonic temple was built with such symbols. Young, *Diversity*, 142 and 144.

[236] *Ibid.*, 145.

[237] Young observes that Ben Sira has only three references to king in his 51 chapters. He thinks that it is due to the irrelevancy of kingship in the times of Ben Sira (200 BCE). *Ibid.*, 147.

conclusion we would have to draw from this evidence is that Qoheleth is a work of pre-exilic wisdom."[238]

In the study of the language of Qoheleth, Young accepts the fact that one might recognize the Mishnaic flavor in its language at first sight. However, he also observes that "nevertheless, Qoheleth contains more of an admixture of 'classical' Hebrew than does the later-attested Mishnaic Hebrew."[239] To him, Qoheleth's use of modified syntax, i.e., usage of noun + participle formula, instead of the standard *waw* consecutives, shows greater simplicity. And so, he prefers to term the language of Qoheleth as "a colloquial variant of the classical literary Biblical Hebrew."[240] The peculiar noun formations, i.e., nouns ending with $-\hat{o}n$[241] are usually considered to be Aramaisms. But *yitrôn* doesn't exist in Aramaic and only appears in Qoheleth and later texts that refers back to Qoheleth.[242] And $-\hat{o}n$ endings are also attested in Moabite proper names (cf. Jud 3:12). So Young argues that "we may see all these are evidences that Qoheleth, besides sharing isoglosses with other dialects, also has a distinct character of his own."[243] The apparent colloquialism in Qoheleth, which is seen in the incongruence of number and gender, irregular use of the

---

[238] *Ibid.*, 148.

[239] Young discusses features like *kebar*, *še-*, *zoh* as characteristic of Mishnaic or Aramaizing. But he feels that in spite of the Mishnaic coloring of the language, it is not identical with Mishnaic language itself. *Ibid.*, 149.

[240] However, there is a great residual of 'classical forms' in Qoheleth he observes. *Ibid.*, 149.

[241] Nouns like *Hesrôn* (1:15), *Yitrôn* (1:3, 2:11, 13, 3:9, 5:8, 15, 7:12, 10:10,11), *Hešbôn* (7:25, 27, 9:10, 7:29), *Kisron* (2:21, 4:4, 5:10), and *Silton* (8:4,8).

[242] BDB, 452.

[243] Young, *Diversity*, 150. *-on* ending nouns are also attested in North Israelite, ex. capital *somron*.

definite article, leads Young to conclude that "Qoheleth represents a less formal variant of Hebrew than the Standard Literary Language."[244] The question of the genre also allows certain freedom of linguistic uniqueness to Qoheleth. Young holds that "[Qoheleth] … represents a literary genre (the personal monologue style) and a type of language (analogous if not related to Mishnaic Hebrew) which is unique in the ancient Hebrew tradition."[245]

He also evaluates the premises of dating of Qoheleth based on its language. Young agrees that Qoheleth is 'strongly Aramaizing and Mishnaizing' but he doesn't conclude that these are due to the post-exilic composition. Young evaluates 25 LBH words in Qoheleth, which were listed by Driver.[246] He concludes that "Driver's evidence for placing Qoheleth with LBH is hardly as decisive as has been assumed during this century... Driver's data is found to be insignificant for dating Qoheleth."[247] Young maintains that the general reading of Qoheleth evokes the environment of pre-exilic monarchic period and the language should not be used to bring ambiguity to this definite hint. Young also addresses the plausible causes behind the peculiar linguistic usage of Qoheleth. He proposes that, like Mishna which was initially an oral tradition but was later compiled into book format, the materials in Qoheleth could have been spoken in a wisdom school setting and later should

---

[244] *Ibid.*, 150.

[245] This view is also compatible with that of Avi Hurvitz who maintains the genre allows certain stylistic variations in the language. "According to the methodology proposed by Hurvitz to date the late biblical texts," young observes that "Qoheleth should not be allowed to be classified with LBH in general." *Ibid.*, 151.

[246] Young, *Diversity*, 152.

[247] *Ibid.*, 154.

have been arranged and handed it over to *a Tanna*[248] to be passed on to the successive generations. According to this view, the language should have been "an intentional part of the anti-traditional message of Qoheleth."[249] Young's this conclusion is well supported by the earlier chapters that elucidates the diversity that co-existed throughout the history of Hebrew language.

Conclusions of Young

In his conclusion, Young emphasizes that the language of Qoheleth should be defined as a "local literary dialect with much greater mixture of classical elements."[250] He emphasizes that the inherent monarchic backdrop of Qoheleth should be taken as the important indicator to point to the pre-exilic dating. This conclusion does not negate the traditional preference for Solomonic authorship. He pertinently observes, "If anyone wished to argue for the traditional Solomonic authorship, the criteria discussed above could not be used against this theory."[251]

Evaluation of Young

The field of *diglossia* in Hebrew language has gained much attention in the recent years. Along the lines of the diachronic development which scholars trace within the extant biblical corpus, the diversity that exists in the language from Hebrew's

---

[248] Tannaim, also known as repeaters, were the group of ancient scholars who preserved the oral tradition of the sacred text. Though the name *tanna* is first attested in the late period (2nd A.D.), this profession should have been much more ancient.

[249] Young also states that "this theory also justifies and explains the collection of divergent material in the book, from collections of proverbs to long discursive material: Qoheleth choose to include whatever material he felt best exemplified his teaching." *Ibid.,* 156.

[250] *Ibid.,* 157.

[251] *Ibid.,* 157.

origin has not been addressed adequately. In this study, following the research trails of Rendsburg, Young makes a strong case, which is in itself a seed for the lasting debate on the current understanding on the chronological development of the Hebrew as ABH, SBH and LBH.

Many of the simplistic assumptions that capture central place in the scholarly world are questioned by Young: The repeatedly-adduced argument of the foreign loanwords is rendered untenable, and so the case of 'Aramaisms' and 'Mishnaisms' as the indicators of late language. The diverse historical origin of Israel allows such possibility to take all of these factors as synchronic features without resorting to diachronic rationalization. His first three chapters bring in massive wealth of information. They clearly point out that Hebrew did not develop from the changes within or only due to later Aramaic influences, but there are so much more diversity coming from the neighboring nations. This is an agreeable view that in such a strategic location, Israel could not have avoided those social interventions and linguistic additions from her diverse neighbors.

Applying the implications of his theory into the study of the language Qoheleth produces a result contrary to the views of the mainstream scholarship. Rendsburg perceives, "there have been several recent attempts to date these two books (Qoheleth and Song of Songs) to the pre-exilic period, so that Young's efforts in this direction do not stand in isolation."[252] However, this would be the first study to reach such conclusion from the perspective of diglossia.

There are criticisms against Young, which mainly concern the absence or lack of reference to the earlier standard works

---

[252] Gary A. Rendsburg, "Review of Young," *Hebrew Studies* 36 (1995), 139.

in the field of Semitic languages. Rendsburg observes this, "Bibliographic note: an occasional work in Modern Hebrew is cited in Young's bibliography, but numerous important works in this language were not utilized."[253] Schmitz points out the vast number of important resources Young could have used.[254] Though the studies referred provides enough base for him to cement his theory, the lack of reference to earlier seminal studies remains a weakness in Young's arsenal.

In spite of the reservations expressed, Young's contribution adds fresh insight into the nature of the development of the Hebrew language in its ANE context. In the words of Rendsburg, "How are we to judge Young's conclusions? Do they result from the evidence at our disposal? The answer, in my opinion: in some cases, yes; in most cases, no...In sum, in so far as this book brings together a wide array of data concerning the early history of Hebrew language and its Northwest Semitic setting, it is a useful work."[255] However, with regard to the dating of Qoheleth, Rendsburg pronounces discretion and caution, "the broad sweeps attempted in this book and the specific dating of Qoheleth and Song of Song will need to be treated critically."[256] It is necessary to have such caution, as Young has only given a workable model to study Qoheleth's language.

---

[253] *Ibid.*, 139.

[254] Philip C. Schmitz, "Review of Young," *CBQ* 57 (1995), 381. Schimitz is somewhat outspoken in his assessment of Young work in the concluding remarks of his review, "compounded with an unsystematic organization of the evidence, a frequently awkward style of writing and lapses of logic, the shortcomings mentioned leave little to interest the serious researcher." *Ibid.*, 381.

[255] Rendsburg: Review of Young, 137, 139-140. He is also excited to see "a fellow scholar grappling with the issues of diglossia and regional dialects." *Ibid.*, 140.

[256] *Ibid.*, 140.

C. L. SEOW, LINGUISTIC EVIDENCE TO THE DATING OF QOHELETH, 1996

Choon-Leong Seow (C. L. Seow)[257] joins the debate on the language of Qoheleth by the publication of his article titled "Linguistic Evidence to the Dating of Qoheleth" in JBL in 1996. The revised version of this article was later integrated into his commentary on Ecclesiastes.[258] It comes at the last of the series of studies that focus on the language of Qoheleth. It draws different conclusion from the assessment of the data at hand.

Methodology

Seow does not outline any statement of methodology *per se*, but it can be deduced from the outline and the structure of the article. The entire article is divided into three major divisions: orthography, foreign influences, Late Hebrew vernacular with a brief introduction and a candid conclusion. Seow employs comparative philology and discusses grammatical-lexical features.

Summary and Analysis

This article begins with the brief review of the studies on the language of Qoheleth from Grotius and the impact of Delitzsch. He observes that the studies of Isaksson, Fredericks and Schoors

---

[257] Seow is Henry Snyder Gehman Professor of Old Testament Language and Literature in Princeton Theological Seminary, NJ. His research interests are in history of Israelite religion, Israelite wisdom literature, Northwest Semitic epigraphy, and the history of biblical interpretation. His publications include *Ecclesiastes* (AB, 1997), *Kings* (NIB, 1999), and *Myth, Drama, and the Politics of David's Dance* (HSM, 1989). Seow serves on the editorial boards of *JBL*, *CBQ*, the SBL Writings in the Ancient World series, and the Abingdon Old Testament Commentary series. C. L. Seow, *PTSEM Faculty Information*: http://www.ptsem.edu/Academics/departments/BS/Faculty/seow.htm (Accessed, October 2, 2009).

[258] C. L. Seow, Ecclesiastes, *AB 18C* (New York: Double Day, 1997).

have reignited the debate. He perceives this development as the reason for him to undertake the current study. He states that "it is necessary now to reconsider the linguistic evidence and the probable date of the book in the light of these new studies."²⁵⁹

The section on orthography, Seow begins addressing the view of Dahood that Qoheleth was originally written in standard Phoenician orthography, without any vowel letters and observes that it has been largely rejected among the scholars. Seow notes that "taking the MT at face value, one might argue that the ample use of internal vowel letters in fact points to an exilic or post exilic date."²⁶⁰ While admitting some orthographic inconsistencies in the book, he also maintains that "such are also found in inscriptions from the post-exilic period."²⁶¹ He also observes the conservative use of internal vowel letters in comparison to the Qumran scrolls where *plene* forms are more common. He concurs that "the use of internal vowel letters is more restricted than what one might expect to find in the Hebrew of Qumran, Wadi Murabba'at and Bar Kochba letters."²⁶² He affirms with Schoors that a middle stage of *plene* writing to be found in Qoheleth.²⁶³ Based on the observations from orthography, he concludes, "if orthographic conventions may be used as a criterion for dating the language, Qoheleth should be placed somewhere between the beginning of the sixth century and the end of the third century BCE."²⁶⁴

---

²⁵⁹ Seow: Linguistic Evidence, 644.

²⁶⁰ He points out certain examples such as the original long *î* being marked by *yod* in Qoheleth (רָאִיתִי, עֲשִׂירִים), masculine plural ending always written with a *yod* (וְהָאֱלֹהִים), etc. *Ibid.*, 645.

²⁶¹ *Ibid.*, 645.

²⁶² *Ibid.*, 646.

²⁶³ *Ibid.*, 646. See also, Schoors, *Pleasing Words I*, 32.

²⁶⁴ *Ibid.*, 646.

Seow further categorizes the foreign language influence on Qoheleth under four sub-divisions: Persianisms, Aramaisms, Phoenicianisms, and Grecisms. Mostly, his comparisons are lexical; and in the case of Grecisms, he also takes into consideration the conceptual resemblances with Greek thought along with alleged influence on the vocabulary. Seow points out that the use of the two Persian words in Qoheleth may have definite bearing upon the dating of Qoheleth. He lists 22 Persian words from the post-exilic books of Chronicles, Esther, Ezra-Nehemiah and Esther and argues that all the Persian words in the Bible are found in the later books. He then concludes, "All occurrences of Persian loanwords and proper names are found in texts postdating the second major wave of returnees in the second half of the fifth century."[265] And so he concludes that, "the existence of these two Persian loanwords in Qoheleth suggests that the book should be dated no earlier than the second half of the fifth century."[266] He moves on to tackle the issue of the "high frequency of Aramaisms" in Qoheleth which had given rise to Aramaic Translation theory. Having rejected translation theory, he supposes that there are many Aramaisms which call for a later date. He lists out 22 lexical references which are attested in imperial Aramaic and he concludes that "these terms are all at home in the economic vocabulary of the Persian Period."[267] His important argument

---

[265] *Ibid.*, 649. The word "פַּרְדֵּסִים" in 2:5 comes from Old Persian *paridaida*. It has attestation from the Persepolis Fortification Tablets as *par-te-tas* "domains" around 500 BCE. Akkadian cognate *pardesu* also is attested from several Babylonian texts from the second half of the sixth century and later. It also has Greek attestation from the 4th BCE. The second word "פִּתְגָם" in 8:11 is derived from the Old Persian word *patigama*, again attested around 500 BCE. It also occurs in BA and later books. See, Daniel 3:16, 4:4, Esth 1:20, Ezra 4:17, Sirach 5:11. *Ibid.*, 649.

[266] *Ibid.*, 650.

[267] *Ibid.*, 651.

is that שלט (2:19, 5:18, 6:2) has the economic nuance of controlling the inheritance and assets.[268] He argues that this legal meaning was not carried on beyond the Persian Period, and [later on] it came to mean having power, etc.[269] Briefly, he concludes that the density of imperial Aramaic influence in Qoheleth's terminology and the case of שלט well justifies "a date no later than the Persian period."[270] He also addresses the probable influence of Phoenician in the syntax and vocabulary as proposed by Dahood. He concludes that all of Dahood's proposals either have precedence in BH or LBH.[271] His conclusion on the Phoenician influence is that "the possibility of some idioms in Qoheleth is a result of Phoenician influences cannot be ruled out... It is suggestive that the idiom ("under the sun") occurs also in Phoenician inscriptions from the fifth century."[272] Seow takes the date of Phoenician inscription to support his Persian period dating.[273] While denying the presence of Greek loanwords, Seow undertakes a survey to see the idioms which are taken by various scholars to be Grecisms. And he firmly concludes that "there are no Greek loanwords in Qoheleth, indeed, no linguistic Grecisms

---

[268] He adduces an ANE reference to the legal document from Elephantine which uses שלט in the same sense "to have the right of disposal."

[269] However, this conclusion was disputed by Rudman. See, Rudman, *Determinism in the Book of Ecclesiastes*, 15.

[270] *Ibid.*, 654.

[271] He observes, "...virtually all of these features are found in Biblical Hebrew, notably in Late Biblical Hebrew." *Ibid.*, 655.

[272] *Ibid.*, 657.

[273] This phrase is attested twice in Phoenician, in the inscriptions of Kings Tabnit and Eshmunazor of Sidon (KAI 13.7-8; 14.12). Seow thinks that "the idiom in Qoheleth may have been borrowed directly from Phoenician although the expression in Phoenician itself may have come from elsewhere." *Ibid.*, 656f.

whatsoever."²⁷⁴ He does not see any attempt for archaism in Qoheleth in opposition to Qumran scrolls.

The next major section titled as "Late Hebrew Vernacular" identifies six morphological variations. He argues that the frequency of שֶׁ, and its various grammatical functions are much characteristic of LBH.²⁷⁵ The exclusive usage of אֲנִי is also taken to indicate the post-exilic date.²⁷⁶ Also, Seow thinks that the usage of אֵת / אֶת in Qoheleth is different from its standard usage in the pre-exilic texts as direct object marker.²⁷⁷ The exclusive use of the feminine demonstrative זֹה also points to the later date. He supposes that the lack of consistency in using masculine endings for the feminine plural nouns is a clear example for the lateness of the language which is not attested in the BH. The negation of the infinitive with אֵין, similar constructions appear in Ben Sira and Post-Exilic works.²⁷⁸ Seow does not take the language as closer to that of Mishna, but "the Hebrew of Qoheleth is like Mishnaic Hebrew only inasmuch as both languages are the literary deposits of popular, everyday speech."²⁷⁹

Conclusions of Seow

His conclusions are quite forthright. His main argument here is that the language of Qoheleth is Post-exilic which is

---

²⁷⁴ *Ibid.*, 660.

²⁷⁵ Seow concludes that "שֶׁ is always used as a relative particle in the older texts, but not to introduce an object or a purpose clause." *Ibid.*, 661.

²⁷⁶ He compares the other texts from late period, such as Haggai, Song of Song, Ezra and Esther which use אֲנִי exclusively to come to this conclusion. *Ibid.*, 661.

²⁷⁷ *Ibid.*, 662.

²⁷⁸ *Ibid.*, 664.

²⁷⁹ *Ibid.*, 665.

warranted by the high frequency of Aramaisms, Persian loanwords, and the economic sense of the word שלט. According to him, "in terms of a typology of language, then Qoheleth belongs in the Persian period, specifically between the second half of the fifth century and the first half of the fourth... it's the literary deposit of a vernacular, specifically the everyday language of the Persian period."[280] He takes the language used in Qoheleth as representative of the spoken dialect, contrary to the standard literary language of Persian era.

Evaluation of Seow

Seow has done a commendable work in his article in summarizing the view of earlier scholarship and also coming to a prompt conclusion based on the study of Qoheleth's vocabulary which, according to him, is at home within the economic common stock of the Persian period. His appreciative tone towards the laborious studies of Dahood that brought to light some of striking similarities shared by both Hebrew and Phoenician, while not subscribing to his theories, is generally missing in the current scholarship.

Seow betrays simplistic circular reasoning when assessing the loanwords and their bearings on dating: all alleged Persian words in the Bible are appearing in the late books, Qoheleth has two Persian words, so Qoheleth should be dated in the Persian period. However, the appearance of a word in a few inscriptions from Persian period does not deny their existence or transmission earlier. If inscriptional evidences are the sole criteria to base dating of a literature, then current scholarship

---

[280] His rationale for this conclusion is that the author was addressing general populace – "the people" (12:9) which necessitated a simplistic language that accounts for the linguistic variations that are different from the Standard Biblical Texts. *Ibid.*, 666.

is left with too limited vocabularies at their disposal. Also Seow mentions the work of Young in a passing footnote, but did not interact with the conclusions of Young that the heterogeneous linguistic traditions which surround the earlier development of Hebrew should be accounted for the loan words. Briefly, "...to give Persian loanwords the final say in deciding the date of a biblical work is completely exceeding the evidence, albeit that this is precisely what has been done in the past."[281] It should be contended that mere comparisons of vocabularies with epigraphic materials are not the sound methodology to date Qoheleth.

Seow's important defense of the Persian period comes from his study of the term *šalît*, as having been used in Qoheleth in an economic sense. This claim was questioned by Rudman who argues, "Qoheleth's use of שלט in its technical sense has several parallels in documents from fourth and fifth century BCE, but this meaning of words derived from the root evidently survived throughout the Hellenistic period and well into the Christian era."[282] Thus the main premise of Seow's thesis is seriously damaged.

Dahood argued for Phoenician influence on the masculine plural suffix with feminine nouns (2:6, 10, 10:9, 11:8, 12: 1). Seow has rejected this proposal and concluded it as the evidence for

---

[281] Young, *Diversity*, 71. In view of Young, "the loan words exhibit an unusual form and the noun has no known Semitic root. We find *Pithgam* to be a common Indo-European word, attested in Greek, Sanskrit and later Iranian dialects. *Ibid.*, 71. Also see, Mats Eskhult, "The Importance of Loanwords in Dating Biblical Hebrew Texts," in *Biblical Hebrew: Studies in Chronology and Typology* (New York: T&T Clark, 2003): 8-23.

[282] Dominic Rudman, "A Note on the Dating of Ecclesiastes," *CBQ* 61 (1999), 52. Also see, Rudman, *Determinism in the Book of Ecclesiastes*, 15.

Late Biblical Hebrew influence in Qoheleth. However, this is a common feature in the Old Testament and "especially characteristic of spoken Hebrew dialect."[283] Also Seow's view that "the high frequency of Aramaisms" accounts for the date in the late post-exilic period is questioned by Mroczek in a recent study.[284]

Seow's extreme dependence on epigraphical materials, lack of interactions with the latest scholarly positions on the language of Qoheleth, and shaky premise of the Persian period economic terminologies in Qoheleth rendered his position vulnerable.

SUMMARY OF THE CHAPTER

The study of Isaksson was the first one to apply structural linguistics to the language of Qoheleth, especially to the study of its verbal forms. He has concluded that the language still remains distant from MH and its intrinsic structure remains within classical BH. Fredericks has called for the earlier consensus into question and strongly supports the early date of Qoheleth into 8th-7th BCE. Schoors have argued in support of the lateness of the language by summarizing and restating the earlier consensus. The surprise entry to the discussion of the language of Qoheleth is that of Young, who considers a wider methodological framework to discuss the language of the book and its contribution to issues such as dating. Seow has argued for the Persian period dating for Qoheleth which did not gain much acceptance in the recent scholarship.

---

[283] Young, *Diversity*, 32. See, Gary A. Rendsburg, *Evidence for a Spoken Hebrew in Biblical Times* [Ph.D. dissertation, New York University, 1980], 52ff.

[284] See, Eva Mroczek, "Aramaisms in Qohelet: Methodological Problems in Identification and Interpretation," *Issues in Hebrew Philology*, Unpublished paper, (2008).

This chapter has summarized and evaluated each of the major studies that were done on the language of Qoheleth since Isaksson. After all the proliferation of the materials, still the answer to the consensus seems to be out of sight. The following chapter will delineate some of the methodological observations that are briefly touched in this chapter.

3
The Language of Qoheleth: Methodological Assessments and Proposals

After two decades of the recent phase of the study on the language of Qoheleth, what has been painstakingly achieved through the diligent scholarly debates is more ambiguity than clarity. This calls into question the implementation of the current methodologies in the study of Qoheleth's language. While no one methodology can do justice to disclose the intentions of the Hebrew text, the combination of methodologies drew out some stimulating facts, information unidentified in the earlier scholarship. However, a methodology that incorporates the latest development in the field of Biblical Hebrew linguistics is due. This chapter focuses its attention on the presentation of three scholarly positions and also presents a critique of the methodologies currently employed in the studying the language of Qoheleth since Isaksson. And the section on Hurvitz is central as his approach continues to influence the diachronic study of Hebrew in general with undeniable implications to the language of

Qoheleth. The heterogeneity of the language of Qoheleth will be discussed briefly in the final section.

GENERAL CONCERNS ON THE RECENT TREND

The realistic observation of Qoheleth, וְאֵין כָּל־חָדָשׁ תַּחַת הַשָּׁמֶשׁ remains more vindicated, even after the passage of two millennia, when read in the context of many years laborious study on the language of Qoheleth itself. The recent scholarly conclusions are more are less the restatements of earlier views, with a wealth of additional insights and information and reassessments. The following sub-divisions of this chapter outline three of the major scholarly positions pertinent to the language of Qoheleth. This chapter will also address the issue of the apparent stalemate and the future trajectory of the language of Qoheleth.

The Three Scholarly Positions

When one retrospectively looks at 1950s Qoheleth scholarship, the debates between the "Three Theories" mark that era.[1] Apparently, the consensus was formed after the position of Gordis. However, the breach in the consensus during the late 1980s led to another wave of studies, resuming the age-old debate. Though the scholarly world is as divided as ever on this enigmatic book today, traces of irreconcilable extremities seem to polarize into three positions with rigidity, plausibly due to their methodological delineations and assumptions. While Hellenistic period dating for Qohelet holds mainstream support, the two other views remain a minority.

---

[1] Here I mean the main theories of the 1950s as 1) Mishnaic Hebrew and Aramaic Influence Theory (as defended by Gordis and mainstream scholarship), 2) Aramaic Translation Theory (as defended by Zimmermann, C.C. Torrey and Ginsburg), 3) Canaanite-Phoenician Influence Theory (M.H. Dahood).

The Pre-Exilic Period View

After a not-so popular attempt by G. L. Archer in 1969 to defend the Solomonic provenance of Qoheleth, no other scholar has risked his credibility to argue for a pre-exilic date for the book of Qoheleth from the language perspective as the general consensus gathered momentum and seemed impregnable to penetrate.[2] However, three recent important studies seriously weakened this consensus as well as have reiterated the affinity of the language of Qoheleth with classical Hebrew and pre-exilic times. They have come to this conclusion from various starting points as well as by implementing different methodologies.

Isaksson's study, which mainly focused on the verbal system of Qoheleth, had questioned the view that Qoheleth's language is closer to that of Mishnaic Hebrew (MH). The importance of Isaksson's study does not rest upon its chronological predictions, but on the conclusions of Qoheleth's verbal system. Isaksson unequivocally concludes that "the language of Qoheleth – of which the verbal system plays a fundamental part – is far from having a mainly MH grammatical foundation. Rather it is obvious that the grammatical foundation is still mainly BH."[3] This conclusion allowed the plausibility that Qoheleth could have been composed earlier contrary to the consensus.

Fredericks' study questioned the Hellenistic period dating based on its language. He "is outspoken" in the conclusions of

---

[2] Bartholomew in his recent commentary favors a Hellenistic period dating, though he considers the identity of the author of secondary importance. Craig Bartholomew, *Ecclesiastes*, BCOT (Grand Rapids: Baker Academic, 2009), 54, 59.

[3] Isaksson, *Studies in the Language of Qoheleth*, 197.

his study.[4] He not only rejects the consensus[5] but also provides a specific pre-exilic time frame to date the book of Qoheleth based on its language. In the words of Fredericks, "Qoheleth's language should not be dated any later than the exilic period, and no accumulation of linguistic evidence speaks against a pre-exilic date...a date in the pre-exilic era, in the eighth or seventh century BCE might be recommended."[6] His conclusions are perceived as open challenge to the consensus.[7]

Young, approaching the language of Qoheleth from a *diglossia* perspective, also takes a significant stand for the pre-exilic dating of the book of Qoheleth. He notes, "Qoheleth represents a less formal variant of Hebrew than the Standard Literary Language."[8] He strongly contends the general classification of Qoheleth with LBH books.[9] From the perspective of diversity, along with the Pre-exilic monarchic environment as presented in the book, Young concludes that the book of Qoheleth should belong to the pre-exilic biblical

---

[4] Here I am borrowing the vocabulary of Schoors. See, *Schoors, Pleasing Words I*, 15.

[5] Fredericks points out that "these criteria (earlier used in dating Qoheleth)... have resulted in a scholarly consensus on a post-exilic date that is invalid." Fredericks, *Qoheleth's Language*, 266.

[6] *Ibid.*, 262-263.

[7] Such concerns are expressed mainly in the books of Schoors, who represents the mainstream consensus. In fact, Schoors perceives the work of Fredericks as a main threat to the consensus, though he treats other's conclusion but with lesser interest. See, Schoors, *Pleasing Words I*, 14-16.

[8] Young, *Diversity*, 150.

[9] *Ibid.*, 151. In spite of the on going debates on the language of Qoheleth, Joosten takes Qoheleth as an undisputable LBH book, which needs to be mentioned here. See, Jan Joosten, "The Distinction Between Classical and Late Biblical Hebrew As Reflected in Syntax." *HS 46* (2005), 329.

corpus.[10] He points more specifically to the late monarchic era to be the period of Qoheleth's composition.[11]

Though these positions have been reached from various methodological perspectives, the conclusion is strongly unambiguous. It is not possible to date the language of Qoheleth later than monarchic period as it is structurally closer to classical Hebrew. This composite position of three scholars, though largely debated, has drawn considerable attention in the recent times and will continue to influence the trajectory of the language studies in the years to come.

The Persian Period View

Delitzsch had placed this book in the Persian Period. He held that "…it (Book of Qoheleth) was written under Persian domination… it was written somewhere within the last century of the Persian kingdom, between Artaxerxes I, Lonimanus (464-424), and Darius Codomannus (335-332): the better days for the Jewish People, of the Persian supremacy under the first five Achaemenids, were past (7:10)."[12] However, succeeding scholarship had moved even further into Hellenistic period in dating Qoheleth from the linguistic perspective.[13]

---

[10] He also reiterated this conclusion in his following writings. See, Ian Young, "Evidence of Diversity in Pre-Exilic Judahite Hebrew," *HS* 38 (1997), 11.

[11] Ian Young, "Biblical Texts Cannot be Dated Linguistically," *HS* 46 (2005), 347-348

[12] F. Delitzsch, *Ecclesiastes, trans. by* M. A. Easton, (Leipzig: Dörffling & Franke, 1875; Edinburgh: Clark, 1877; reprint, Grand Rapids: Eerdmans, 1982; Peabody, Massachusetts: Hendrickson, 1996), 653-654.

[13] G. A. Barton places Qoheleth in "the last of the third and the beginning of the second century BCE." Barton, *Ecclesiastes*, 62. Gordis opts for a date in the middle of the third century BCE. R. Gordis, *Koheleth – The Man and His World*, 68.

Seow defends the Persian period dating for Qoheleth. He observes that the evidences from Qoheleth's orthography, presence of the Persian words, high frequency of Aramaisms, economic nuance of Qoheleth's vocabularies, absence of Grecisms, as well as typology of language, all leading to an inescapable conclusion of Persian era dating for Qoheleth. He firmly asserts that, "Qoheleth belongs in the Persian Period, specifically between the second half of the fifth century and the first half of the fourth *(450 BCE - 350 BCE)*."[14] At present, Seow's view for the Persian period dating remains a minority view with only a few defending the Persian period dating for Qoheleth.[15]

The Hellenistic Period View
Following the research trails of Barton, Gordis and others, Antoon Schoors has presented a comprehensive defense for the Hellenistic dating of Qoheleth in his two volumes study on the language of Qoheleth. Schoors' study affirmed most of the earlier arguments that were adduced in defense of the Hellenistic dating of Qoheleth.

His conclusions are stated at the end of his two volumes. He acknowledges and reiterates the lateness of the language of Qoheleth and legitimizes placing Qoheleth along with LBH books that are "post-exilic such as Chr, Ezr, Neh, Dan, Sir, or at least exilic Ez, Dt-Isa, or the P texts in the Pentateuch."[16] In

---

[14] Years are inserted and emphasis added.

[15] Kugel also supports the Persian period dating, but not from a linguistic point of view. See, James L. Kugel, "Qoheleth and Money," *CBQ 51/1* (1989): 32-49.

[16] Schoors, *Pleasing words I*, 222. But, Joosten argues that the entire Pentateuch, including the 'P' texts, falls into Classical Biblical Hebrew corpus. He paraphrases Delitzsch's quote and says, "If the Pentateuchal texts were of post-exilic origin, then there is no history of the Hebrew language." Joosten: The Distinction, 339.

his second volume on vocabulary, he builds upon his earlier conclusion from Vol. 1, "the lexical study of this book shows again that the language of Qoh is definitely late in the development of BH and belongs to LBH."[17] He sees Greek parallels in the content, though not in vocabulary and syntax. He notes, "the few acceptable parallels may strengthen the force of Greek parallels in the domain of contents and thus be favorable to a date in the Hellenistic period."[18] However, except this passing hint for Hellenistic preference, there is no explicit reference to a date in all of his two volumes, which has been criticized.[19]

The Perceived Stalemate

The maze of scholarly works on the language of Qoheleth points to the dreary fact that a lot of the arguments that are being used are recycling of earlier materials. While the works of Isaksson and Fredericks can be said to have incorporated new insights into the discussion of the language of Qoheleth, Schoors has mainly majored in gathering the vast amount of data at his disposal that argued for the late date for Qoheleth and had ingeminated them in masterful order to sustain the consensus.

---

[17] Schoors, *Pleasing Words II*, 499-502.

[18] *Ibid.*, 501. See also, A. Schoors, "Qoheleth: A Book in a Changing Society," *Old Testament Essays* 9/1 (1996): 68-87. In this essay, he agrees with "the date in the second half of the third century BCE" along with Gordis and mainstream scholarship. *Ibid.*, 72.

[19] Rogland has been quite harsh on this point of Schoors not taking a specific stand at the end of his two comprehensive volumes on the language of Qoheleth: "Where else ought one to make a case for the date of Qoheleth's language, if not after a five-hundred-page study of the book's vocabulary, which itself follows an over two-hundred-page study of its grammar? In the end, one gets the feeling that one has been chasing the wind all along, which is indeed a vexation and a grievous evil under the sun!" See, Max Rogland, Review of Schoors, "Pleasing Words II," *RBL* 02 (2006): 1-5.

It can be clearly seen in Schoors rejecting of some of the arguments of Fredericks by merely attesting the authority of the earlier studies, than by engaging them in discussion with the texts in contrast.[20]

It has become increasingly clear that there is a traceable development among Biblical linguists, who perceive for granted, that the debate on the language of Qoheleth is closed. The majority of the scholars, who hold the diachronic view that Qoheleth's language belongs to the LBH corpus, begin to treat it like it's an undisputedly established LBH book, in spite of their knowledge that the debate is still raging. Such scholarly insensitiveness to the current trend on the debate is unacceptable the least and questionable at best.[21]

In terms of the freshness of the approach, Young's view of diglossia has questioned the mere comparison of the lexical, syntactical reflexes within the biblical corpus and with the epigraphical references. This approach, with slight

---

[20] See, *Schoors Pleasing words I*, Note 290-291; 283-284; 387-388. Moreover, large numbers of Schoors' footnotes, that are being repeatedly adduced to support the lateness of Qoheleth's language, are from Delitzsch (1875), G. C. Aalders (1948), Gordis (1951), and so on. It's an irony worth noting: even though Schoors considers the main breach on the consensus was caused by Fredericks and giving an impression that his study is going to be a serious response to that of Fredericks, one finds that it's more or less a serious defense against the theory of Dahood at many junctures. It might puzzle the readers: for, why would someone want to go into laborious depths to disqualify a theory that had already been abandoned for decades and virtually absent in contemporary scholarship?

[21] Hurvitz refers to Ecclesiastes as a LBH book in his 1973 article. This might be sustainable in light of the prevailing consensus of that time. However, continuing such sentiments into the current scholarship should be avoided as the debate on Qoheleth's linguistic affinity and date is yet to be established. See, Avi Hurvitz, "Linguistic Criteria for Dating Problematic Biblical Texts," *HA* 14 (1973): 74-79. Also, Joosten: The Distinction, 329.

modifications in the methodological contour, holds promise to enlightening the issue. At the moment, the weary conclusion of Isaksson might be the best to agree with, "If we find within the biblical period a clearly datable new Hebrew document of a philosophical-sapiential kind, I predict it will revolutionize the Qoheleth research"[22] –a perceptive statement that succinctly encapsulates the passivity in the current studies on Qoheleth's language.

Will the Riddle of the Sphinx Ever Be Resolved?

Not only are there varieties of views on interpreting the theological outlook of Qoheleth, but even within the framework of the studies on its language, it is a legitimate question to raise: will the riddle of the Sphinx ever be resolved? The main reason for resorting to the linguistic argument to understand the problematic text is the lack of definite historical references. The linguistic criterion is the plausible objective method to identify the period of such writings. Such assumptions are quite fundamental to the diachronic study of Biblical linguistics which has caught the central stage in biblical scholarship in the post historical-critical era.[23] Joosten observes, "the criterion of language stands out for its precision and function as a control to the other approaches."[24] And Hurvitz expresses a similar attitude that "we believe that it is this linguistic aspect which

---

[22] Isaksson, *Studies in the language of Qoheleth*, 197

[23] The scholars who significantly influenced the field of the diachronic study of Biblical Hebrew are Avi Hurvitz, Robert Polzin, Gary A. Rendsburg and Frank H. Polak. Also those students who wrote their doctoral dissertations under these scholars often expanded on their diachronic methodological principles. See, Ian Young and Robert Rezetko, *Linguistic Dating of Biblical Texts, Vol. 1* (London: Equinox, 2008), 10-33. The methodological principles of Hurvitz and Polzin, termed as "Hurvitz-Polzin Paradigm" continues to insert influence.

[24] Joosten: The Distinction, 327.

should be primarily studied in order to gain objective criteria for solving chronological issues."[25] Ideally, this might be true. But, can we apply such methodology indiscriminately to all the texts? It is a hard question to answer. As Schniedewind observes, "diachronic analysis is complicated by many social factors."[26]

In view of current Qoheleth scholarship, the polarity in the scholarly positions has rendered such optimism to find consensus by applying this 'so-called' objective linguistic model literally unfeasible. Young argues that the criterion of language should be taken along with theology, theme and content of the book in determining the period of literature.[27] According to him, "linguistic evidence alone is not able to date biblical texts."[28] More importantly, it may be a hard verdict upon texts like Qoheleth where direct historical references are absent and the allusions are obscure to connect with historical events and persons.

Also, Ehrensvärd points out an important factor to ponder in the process. He notes, "this evidence (from biblical Hebrew) is more problematic since later redaction and scribal modification influenced the biblical texts."[29] He also goes on

---

[25] Hurvitz: Linguistic Criteria for Dating Problematic Biblical Texts, 74.

[26] William M. Schniedewind, "Steps and Missteps in the Linguistic Dating of Biblical Hebrew," *HS* 46 (2005), 379.

[27] Young calls linguistic evidence as "evidence" and doesn't attach supreme importance to it. His conclusion is intriguing, "linguistic evidence is evidence, but it is not strong enough on its own to compel scholars to reconsider an argument made on non-linguistic grounds." Ian Young, "Biblical Texts Cannot Be Dated Linguistically," *HS* 46 (2005), 351.

[28] *Ibid.*, 341.

[29] Martin Ehrensvärd, "Why Biblical Texts Cannot Be Dated Linguistically," *HS* 47 (2006), 177.

to point out that "Biblical Hebrew language scholars generally do not pay enough attention to this fact."[30] In the milieu of the current scholarship on Qoheleth's language, the answer to the question whether the riddle of the Sphinx, that has defied the grueling labors of scholars across centuries, could be disclosed through the implementation of the linguistic models seems not so optimistic.

METHODOLOGICAL *IMPASSE*

The circularity and repetitions of scholarly citations, adduced arguments as well as the inability to reach concrete conclusions, as seen in the earlier section of this thesis, point to a certain stagnation within the studies in the language of Qoheleth. The fundamental reasons for such hibernation are to be traced to the methodology of each study. This section will briefly analyze and spell out the inadequacies of current methodologies employed in the study of the language of Qoheleth. The methodology of Hurvitz will be expounded in detail as its principles are at the heart of the flourishing field of the diachronic study of Biblical Hebrew. The final section will attempt to suggest a paradigm that will take into consideration the criticisms of the contemporary models.

Inadequacies of Current Methodologies

This section will discuss four methodologies that are employed in studying the language of Qoheleth, namely structural linguistics, lexical-grammatical analysis, comparative philology and diglossia model. Each methodology brings in a wealth of information that is pivotal in understanding, *inter alia*, the linguistic idiosyncrasies of Qoheleth from various angles.

---

[30] He supposes that "the linguistic profiles of the texts we have may not be that of the original authors. Therefore we must use the evidence with caution." *Ibid.*, 177.

However, such strengths are not to be taken without perceiving the weaknesses of those methodologies under discussion. This section is not attempting the wholesale rejection of the earlier methodologies as inadequate. But it is focused on evaluating their limitations in scope.

Structural Linguistics

The application of structural linguistics to Qoheleth by Isaksson was a major step forward in Qoheleth studies. While beginning with the workable assumption that every author expresses his thought in the language of his time, Isaksson established the differences between spoken speech (*la parole*) and the core structure of the language (*la langue*) which naturally led him to assert that internal verbal structures are subjected to gradual change. However, as structuralism in itself is a synchronic methodology, it puts Isaksson in a crossroad predicament not to draw diachronic conclusions from his synchronically done analysis. And when he had to make the prediction of date, which was well beyond his scope, he did so with a lot of reluctance. Also, the importance of structuralism is seen in the study of phonemics and individual speech units, and not so much in the syntaxes (sentence structure as a whole). So, while Isaksson was successful in analyzing individual features of Qoheleth's language, the lacking of overarching syntactical analysis is a notable weakness of this approach. To be brief, this methodology helped Isaksson to analyze the Qoheleth's pattern of language usage within the text itself. It has not taken a broad approach to the language of Qoheleth in general and did not pay much attention to other factors such as genre, dialect, etc.

Lexical-Grammatical Analysis

The diachronic study of Biblical Hebrew was initially developed from a close study of the lexicon.[31] So, lexical examinations capture central emphasis in most of the studies that are done in biblical diachrony. Also, the importance of analyzing grammatical features found a key place in such studies due to the rationale that grammatical features are very resistant to change in comparison to the lexical elements. Fredericks and Schoors begin with this assumption that the language of Qoheleth can be related to some period within the history of Hebrew language, and thus their methodology has to be related with the diachronic model.

One of the main problems with this methodology is that it seeks to explain the differences in forms, morphological variations, lexical idiosyncrasies as well as grammatical alternatives as chronologically significant and looks for resemblances of such expressions, vocabularies in the extant biblical and/or post-biblical corpus of Hebrew language. The importances of style, dialectal influence, authorial preferences for genre purposes, etc., are not incorporated within this model sufficiently. While Fredericks attempts to incorporate the elements of style, influence of genre, etc into this methodology, Schoors had remained skeptical of such features as they might lead to more subjective suppositions, beyond warranted by the methodology itself.

Comparative Philology

Seow utilized a methodology closer or akin to comparative philology, currently known as Comparative Linguistics, which

---

[31] Joosten observes that "the most impressive illustrations of diachronic development in biblical Hebrew come from the lexicon." Joosten: The Distinction, 328. Also see, Hurvitz, "The Recent Debate on the Late Biblical Hebrew: Solid Data, Experts Opinions and Inconclusive Arguments," *HS* 47 (2006), 202.

is one of the branches of historical linguistics.³² Again, Seow's methodology was also driven by diachronic outlook. At the end of each of his sections, he repeatedly draws diachronic conclusions, though superfluous at times. One of the problematic conclusions is that of orthography.³³ He also repeatedly adduces the high frequency argument for LBH words against which S. R. Driver issued a warning more than a century ago.³⁴

According to Seow, the very presence of the two Persian loanwords in Qoheleth also seems to affirm the Persian period dating, a method which has been under serious criticisms in recent times.³⁵ Moreover, he repeatedly refers to epigraphic as well as post-biblical references to point to the lateness of the date of Qoheleth's language. Currently, the inconsistency of epigraphic attestations is gaining much more than cursory treatments in scholarly discussions. Young points out to "the

---

³² This methodology is used to compare two or more different languages to determine their historical connections. And this is also used to reconstruct various obscure words in comparison to a close cognate language.

³³ Seow treats orthography as a chronological identifier. But the recent trend in the studies of orthography treats them as chronologically unstable and attributes the variations to scribal transmissional factors. Joosten accepts that "orthographic changes are linguistically irrelevant." And Zevit affirms this notion, "the problem of orthography doesn't belong to the linguistic repertoire, but clearly has to do with the editing of the text." See, Ziony Zevit, "Symposium Discussion Session: An Edited Transcription." *HS* 46 (2005): 376.

³⁴ The age-old warning of Driver to the biblical Hebraists, "to guard against a mechanical use of the concordance and not to be carried away by the frequency argument without weighing them in their context." S. R. Driver, "On Some Alleged Affinities of the Elohist," *Journal of Philology* 11 (1882), 203-217. Such caution is also expressed by Hurvitz. Also see, Hurvitz: The Recent Debate, 202.

³⁵ Young writes, "Gone are the days when we could argue confidently from a single Persian loanword that a book must have been composed in the Persian period. Individual linguistic elements in the text come and go in scribal transmission." Young: Biblical Texts, 350-351.

large gap in our external sources for Hebrew between the last inscriptions dated to the early sixth century BCE and the first DSS in the third century BCE."[36] However, Seow nonchalantly substantiates the authority of his dating preference without referring to any such methodological difficulties in the process of dating Qoheleth. The examples of Late Hebrew vernacular that he adduces are all identified to be well within the use of Biblical Hebrew. Seow's methodology suffers much from lack of recognizing the synchronic variants as well as elements such as the underlying influence of genre and style. He seems to be in a hasty pre-occupation to find the resonance of Qoheleth's lexical elements within the Persian period Hebrew.

The Diglossia Model

The diglossia methodology holds that, "two synchronic varieties of one language are used for different purposes, one for formal communication (e.g., the majority of literature), the other for colloquial purposes (e.g., the language of the home)"[37] at the same time. It also holds that linguistic diversity entered Hebrew as it "absorbed a number of non-Judahite elements" from the co-existing diverse people groups. [38] This approach agrees that there was a chronological development in the history of Hebrew language.[39] But, it is suspicious that evidences for such chronological developments are found

---

[36] *Ibid.*, 344.

[37] Young: Evidence of Diversity, 8.

[38] *Ibid.*, 8. See also, I. Young, "The Northernisms of Israelite Narratives in Kings," *ZAH 8* (1995), 69.

[39] Young remarks thoughtfully on the issue of SBH/LBH debate, "Standard Hebrew and Late Hebrew exist. How late does standard Hebrew go? How early does late Hebrew go? It is not that there isn't a development here and there.. it does not compel me to chronological conclusions." Zevit: Symposium, 374.

within the biblical corpus and views the tripartite division of the Hebrew language into ABH, SBH and LBH as diglossia.[40] Such emphasis on the simultaneous existence of linguistic variety is pitched hard against the diachronic model.[41]

While this methodology casts an insightful light on the issues that are either completely ignored or marginalized (linguistic diversity, bearing of genre on the language, among others), it has been too adamant to accept even the reasonable diachronic developments from the pre-exilic as well as post-exilic biblical books. Total rejection of the diachronic approach doesn't seem to be a healthy way forward either. For, all the late features cannot be explained only by means of synchronic variations, as ably shown by Hurvitz.[42]

Observations on the Hurvitz-Polzin Paradigm[43]
Generally scholars recognize the fact that Hurvitz's contribution to the development of the diachronic model has been very significant in recent decades.[44] His methodology,

---

[40] Kutscher introduced this method of identifying changing linguistic patterns within Hebrew. And it is mostly followed by the current scholarship. See, Young, *Biblical Hebrew*, 3.

[41] Young following the trails of Rendsburg has been successful in developing this methodology along with Rezetko, Ehrensvärd and others. Young argues that "not only did SBH continue to be written in post-exilic period, but LBH linguistic features were already in existence at least in late monarchic period." Young: Biblical Texts, 347.

[42] Hurvitz: The Recent Debate, 195-210.

[43] Zevit uses this phrase in his presentation at NAPH session (National Association of Professors of Hebrew) that met during 2005 SBL meeting and a year later the same was published in *Hebrew Studies*. This describes the current trend in biblical studies well. See, Ziony Zevit, "What a Difference a Year Makes: Can biblical texts be dated linguistically?" *HS 47* (2006), 89.

[44] Rooker pays his respect as he observes that, "the individual, who has unquestionably contributed the most to the diachronic study of Biblical Hebrew, certainly in the last quarter of the twentieth century,

well-complimented and reinforced by that of Polzin, has been solely and widely used by the defendants of diachronic methodology to study the chronological significance of various linguistic features found across the Biblical corpus.[45] This section discusses the basic principles that are foundational to this methodology with an concise evaluation at the end.

The Methodological Rationale of Hurvitz

Hurvitz's methodology is, in general, appreciated for its emphasis on objective examination of texts. He recognized the subjectivity of earlier methods for dating problematic texts and the pressing need for having stricter criteria which promises impartial results. He voiced his concern as follows:

> "Unfortunately, the *theological*, *historical* and *literary* criteria which have been used for establishing the date of chronologically problematic texts are very often subjective. Linguistic studies likewise did not produce satisfactory results, since they were not usually based upon methodologically reliable criteria."[46]

---

is Avi Hurvitz, a student of Kutscher's..." Mark F. Rooker, "Diachronic Analysis and the Features of Late Biblical Hebrew," *BBR* 4 (1994), 136. Young respectfully notes, "In recent decades, the contribution of Avi Hurvitz to this field has outweighed all his contemporaries. In numerous books and articles, he has advanced and, indeed, shaped the current discourse on the topic of diachronic variation in BH." Young, *Biblical Hebrew*, 1.

[45] Zevit gives the example for a situation where the combination of Hurvitz-Polzin paradigm was applied and tested. Zevit: What a Difference, 86-87. It is said that Polzin's monograph went on to become "the most widely cited publication on Late Biblical Hebrew in general." Young and Rezetko, *Linguistic Dating of Biblical Texts*, 25. See, R. Polzin, *Late Biblical Hebrew: Toward an Historical Typology of Biblical Hebrew Prose* (Missoula: Scholars, 1976).

[46] Hurvitz: Linguistic Criteria, 74.

This identification of the crisis as well as formulating sound methodology led him to verbalize his own. His assumptions and rationale show reservations in dating a problematic text hastily to a particular diachronic period based on scantly attested linguistic features. However, it is axiomatic that he was sure about the linguistic differences of Hebrew in the pre-exilic period and post-exilic period; without such assumption at the core, Hurvitz's methodology does not stand. The four pillars of Hurvitz's paradigm are briefly summarized, as found in his 1973 article that delineated its essence: [47]

1. The element should appear only, or mainly, in such Biblical books as Daniel, Ezra or Esther; i.e., in books which all scholars accept as late (Late Frequency).

2. There should be alternative elements found in earlier books which express the same meaning (Linguistic Opposition).

3. The element in question should be vital (in regular use) in post-exilic sources other than LBH (= Late BH) – for instance, in BA (= Biblical Aramaic) or MH (= Mishnaic Hebrew) (External sources as controls).

4. The text will not be considered late unless it manifests numerous late elements – one or two isolated examples can always be interpreted as a coincidence (Linguistic Accumulation).

He also outlined a similar methodology for determining the chronological significance of Aramaisms in BH.[48] This

---

[47] *Ibid.*, 76-77.

[48] Hurvitz is against the simplistic conclusion that the very presence of Aramaisms point to the later date for any biblical literature. Hurvitz, "The Chronological Significance of Aramaisms in Biblical Hebrew," 234 – 240; "Hebrew and Aramaic in the Biblical Period: The Problem of Aramaisms in Linguistic Research of the Hebrew Bible," in *Biblical Hebrew*: 34-37.

methodology became the sole underlying principle in all of his writings as well as those scholars defending diachronic dating of biblical texts after him.[49]

Major Conclusions of Hurvitz-Polzin

Hurvitz's inherent premise is that the languages of pre-exilic biblical books are linguistically varied from that of the post-exilic books and that the earlier vocabularies and constructions functioned with expanded semantics and grammatical horizons. He perceives the Babylonian exile as a definite influential factor in the chronological development of Hebrew language.[50] He terms the language of Pre-exilic Hebrew as SBH (Standard Biblical Hebrew = Classical / Early Biblical Hebrew) and the language of Post-exilic Hebrew as LBH (Late Biblical Hebrew). The end of SBH is pointed to be around 6th century BCE.[51] And the book of Ezekiel is identified with the transitional kind of Hebrew that stands between SBH to LBH.[52] And so, the Pentateuch and the former prophets (up to the Book of Kings) are said to be written in SBH and belongs to the period before 500 BCE, and books like Chronicles, Ezra-Nehemiah, Esther are said to contain typical LBH forms and features that belong chronologically to a later period. His study focuses mainly on the lexical features that appear in SBH books and contrasts them with that in the LBH corpus and vice-versa in

---

[49] The basic premises of Hurvitz methodology has remained constant and been sustained with predominant support until Young's criticism in the recent times.

[50] Hurvitz: The Recent Debate, 191.

[51] Avi Hurvitz, "Evidence of Language in Dating the Priestly Code: A Linguistic Study in Technical Idioms and Terminology." *Revue Biblique* 81 /1 (1974), 26.

[52] Avi Hurvitz, *A Linguistic Study of the Relationship of the Priestly source and the Book of Ezekiel*, Cahiers de la Revue Biblique (Paris: Gabalda, 1982), 113.

order to determine their chronological placement. His main foundation was lexicographical, rather than grammatical.[53]

Robert Polzin undertook an *ambitious*[54] study of mainly tracing 19 grammatical features in Chronicles, and P, in sections from Pentateuch, former prophet, Esther and Ezra-Nehemiah to determine their Chrono-linguistic placement within the Biblical corpus. He proposed the order of biblical books based on their linguistic profiles, i.e., based on the frequency of such LBH features in these books: more the congruency, the book was identified with LBH; lesser the congruency, it was attributed to Classical Hebrew (JE, Dtr, and the Court History). He identified P with transitional Hebrew and Chronicles as an example of LBH. Like Hurvitz, he also began his research with the assumption that exile had serious repercussions on Hebrew language. In many points, he affirms the works of Hurvitz, with regards to Aramaisms, the traceability of the linguistic development within the biblical corpus, among others.

However, the main focus of Polzin's work remained on grammatical foundations, which he rightfully rationalized as more objective than the lexicographical features.[55] While Hurvitz cites Ezekiel as an example for transitional Hebrew, Polzin finds the transitional character in P. In view of the language of the inscriptions such as Lachish and Arad Ostraca, Polzin takes them to be closer to LBH (but Hurvitz places them

---

[53] Zevit observes about the emphasis of Hurvitz, "he settled primarily on a contrastive analysis of lexical items and some syntax..." Zevit: What a difference, 85. Also, see note.8 in Joosten: The Distinction, 329.

[54] Quoting the words of Zevit here: "complementing Hurvitz's early lexicographical work, was a single, ambitious study by Robert Polzin." *Ibid.*, 86.

[55] Polzin remarked, "it appears to me that grammatical/syntactical features are more efficient chronological indicators than are lexical features.." Polzin, *Late Biblical Hebrew*, 15f, 123f.

in late monarchic-era, at the end of First Temple Period). Polzin does not detect any archaizing tendencies in Chronicles, Ezra and Nehemiah [2] [56] where as Hurvitz affirms various degrees of arachaisation in all LBH books. Regardless of these differences, the working methodologies and the conclusions of these two scholars have provided a solid foundation for the subsequent studies which were mainly emphasizing the diachronic developments of Hebrew language within biblical books.

An Evaluation of Hurvitz-Polzin Paradigm
Though the methodology of Hurvitz was meticulously prepared, its central emphasis was upon the lexical elements. And it was found wanting while trying to demonstrate the lateness of books such as Haggai and Zachariah, as these books shows greater resemblance to the language of Pre-exilic times.[57] Polzin's approach based on the levels of congruence-incongruence, also dated Zachariah to the date of P^g corpus, not along side Chronicles or Ezra or N[2].[58] Such methodologically inconsistent results evoked the need for sharpening these methodologies or structuring new paradigms.

Hurvitz-Polzin's studies were all conducted in narrative prose of Chronicles, Former prophets, Esther, Ezra-Nehemiah, Ezekiel, etc. There was no complete treatment of the language of Qoheleth, nor did any other poetical books receive

---

[56] Generally, N^2 identified with Nehemiah 7.6 – 12.26. N^1 is identified with Nehemiah 1.1-7.5; 12.27-13:31.

[57] Zevit: What a Difference, 86.

[58] A. E. Hill argued that Polzin's methodology couldn't date Zachariah to the post-exilic period. See, A. E. Hill, "Dating Second Zachariah: A Linguistic Reexamination," *HAR* 6 (1982): 114 -131.

comprehensive treatment based on Hurvitz-Polzin paradigm.[59] But ironically, as Qoheleth reflects some of the "proposed late features" both in grammatical as well as lexicographical levels, it has been taken for granted that Qoheleth should be counted along with LBH books. In fact, it is worth noting that Qoheleth is the only book which has a semi prosaic-poetical language in comparison to the other books that are currently marked as LBH corpus. It seems like such distinctions have not received due attention. Another important factor to consider is the nature of the book of Qoheleth. It is the only philosophical work of this kind in the Bible. While Chronicles had a definite early referral point in the books of Samuel-Kings, Qoheleth has been repeatedly referred to only in the post-biblical book like Ben Sira.[60] Qoheleth is a unique philosophical-sapiential composition within the Biblical corpus. The Hurvitz-Polzin paradigm that works based on the "earlier-later" comparison of language features can not satisfactorily explain the peculiarities of the language of Qoheleth as it has no early point of reference to contrast within the Biblical corpus.

A serious criticism of this paradigm has to do with its somewhat fanatical emphasis upon the chronological conclusion for linguistic variations in the text. This approach, *ipso facto*, denies the plausibility that a biblical author could have employed a peculiar language for a specific reason, and confine the texts strictly within the world of a chronological stratum. This issue has been ably raised by Young and Rezetko,

---

[59] Hurvitz had responded to Young's non-chronological proposal in his recent article on Qoheleth's language. It's a limited lexical study, not a comprehensive study on Qoheleth's language. See, Avi Hurvitz, "The Language of Qoheleth and Its Historical Setting within Biblical Hebrew," in *The Language of Qoheleth in context* (Leuven: Peeters, 2007): 23-34. Also see, J. Joosten, "The Syntax of Volitive Verbal Forms in Qoheleth in Historical Perspective," in in *The Language of Qoheleth in context* (Leuven: Peeters, 2007): 47 - 61.

[60] See, Fredericks, *Qoheleth's Language*, 111-117.

"Is chronology the only or best explanation for linguistic variety in biblical texts? To what degree do other (strictly speaking) non-chronological factors, such as dialect and diglossia, account for the different linguistic profiles of biblical texts?"[61] There should be space for allowing such flexibility, which is not plausible, within the current paradigm of Hurvitz-Polzin. Ironically, the assumed objectivity of this methodology turns out to be its inevitable 'Achilles heel' as well.

From the perspective of the chronological Hebrew model, it is being widely believed that the extra-biblical inscriptions and epigraphical materials from various periods from the history of Hebrew languages serve as external controls to date the Biblical books into various periods. [62] Such delineations underlie not only the earlier works but are also found as part of Hurvitz's methodology itself.[63] The assumption that

---

[61] Young and Rezetko, *Linguistic Dating of Biblical Texts*, 3.

[62] William James Adams Jr., and L. La Mar Adams state that "since the dating of the parts of the Old Testament is much debated, it was decided *to analyze all available Hebrew inscriptions which date to Old Testament times as control text."* [*Emphasis added*]. Their idea that Hebrew was replaced by Aramaic as a vernacular during the post-exilic period is now abandoned. Currently, Hebrew was believed to have been spoken well into the first C.E. They were so confident that the inscriptions point to the certain chronological periods in the history Hebrew language: a) Early date level (900-700 BC) – Mesha Stone, Siloam Inscription, Samaritan Calendar; b) Middle date level (700-586 BC) – Lachish Letters, Arad Ostraca, etc; c) Late date level (586-458 BC) – no inscriptions; d)very late level (458-100 BC) – Manual of Discipline and DSS. William James Adams Jr., L. La Mar Adams, "Language Drift and The Dating of Biblical Passages," *HS* 18 (1977), 160-164. Such optimism is no more plausible in current scholarship, especially with regards to the epigraphic materials.

[63] Hurvitz argued, "... [Non-biblical] sources provide us with the external control required in any attempt to detect and identify diachronic developments within BH.... by and large, there is a far-reaching linguistic uniformity underlying both the pre-exilic inscriptions

epigraphical Hebrew corresponds to the biblical Hebrew of various periods was challenged recently.[64] Young holds that the inscriptions show a more diverse linguistic stratum than BH in general. More important is his observation on the scarcity of inscriptions, "Inscriptional Hebrew is best seen as an independent corpus within ancient Hebrew... there is a large gap in our external sources for Hebrew between the last inscriptions dated to the early sixth century BCE., and the first Dead Sea Scrolls in the third century BCE."[65] If that is accepted, then the external epigraphic controls become quite a shaky place to affirm the texts of the Bible as early or late, which in turn deprives the Hurvitz methodology from its important pillar. The above mentioned critics recognize the important methodological flaw within the diachronic model of linguistic dating. And employing this model to evaluate the language of

---

and the literary biblical texts written in Classical BH." Avi Hurvitz, "The Historical Quest for "Ancient Israel" and the Linguistic Evidence of the Hebrew Bible: Some Methodological Observations," *VT* 47/3 (1997), 307-308. This similar idea is also found in his methodology, point 3. Rooker, following Hurvitz asserted that "the observations from linguistic contrast and linguistic distribution] may be reinforced when extra-biblical parallels from the Dead Sea Scrolls or rabbinic materials are considered." Rooker: Diachronic Analysis, 137.

[64] For the comprehensive treatment of extra-biblical inscriptions, see Young, *Diversity*, 97-121. I. Young, "The Style of the Gazer Calendar and Some "Archaic Biblical Hebrew Passages," *VT XLII*, 3 (1992): 362 – 375. I. Young, "Late Biblical Hebrew and Hebrew Inscriptions" in *Biblical Hebrew*, 276-311. I. Young, "Evidence of Diversity in Pre-exilic Judahite Hebrew," *HS 38* (1997), 8. Young makes this perceptive observation, "we should not, of course, dogmatically assert that the inscriptions give us the full range of possible early Hebrews. Nevertheless, the best reading of the evidence at hand would place the Bible in its current form no earlier than the Persian period... However, one should hesitate to draw far reaching conclusions on the basis of such meager evidence." Young: Late biblical Hebrew and Hebrew Inscriptions, 310-311.

[65] Young: Biblical Texts, 344.

Qoheleth in itself is unsound and insufficient, and thus incapable of producing any decisive results.

THE LANGUAGE OF QOHELETH AS HETEROGENEOUS

This section discusses the heterogeneity of the language of Qoheleth. Some of the features that are identified as archaic and late in the earlier scholarship will be briefly listed and then a case for genre, colloquialism and diglossia upon the language of Qoheleth will be presented. This section also concludes with suggestions for constructing an integrative methodology which should move beyond the standard chronological model and should be inclusive towards these important factors which are mentioned above.

Archaic and Late Features in Qoheleth

The usage of the phrases such as 'Archaic as well as Late features' are mainly presented here to show the complexity that exists within the language of Qoheleth both in lexical as well as the grammatical level. It is an axiomatic reality while carefully investigating the various features of the language of Qoheleth. The amalgamation of these linguistic features renders the process of identifying Qoheleth with a certain historical period at least impossible to attain.

Archaic Features

The particle הִנֵּה has been largely used in BH in comparison to the LBH books. It primarily functioned within the narratives of Pentateuch and Former prophets to supplement the presentation with more graphic visual emphasis.[66] Eskhult

---

[66] The functions of הִנֵּה is summarized by Tamar Zevit as presentatives. She differentiates between הִנֵּה with suffix and without suffix. While הִנֵּה with suffix occurs with verbs of sight, introducing content clauses, הִנֵּה without suffix appears with אָמַר, and introduces direct speech. Tamar Zevit, "The Particles הִנֵּה and וְהִנֵּה in Biblical

points out that "*wᵉhinnç* represents a visual perception of some circumstance and hence lends more liveliness to the description."⁶⁷ Ehrensvärd provides the statistics of the presence of הִנֵּה in BH with the observation that the frequency of use remains higher in the EBH.⁶⁸ In Qoheleth הִנֵּה appears six times (1:14, 1:16, 2:1, 2:11, 4:1, 5:17), both of the forms with and without the suffix are attested in Qoheleth.⁶⁹

The orthography of the name דָּוִד is important to observe in Qoheleth.⁷⁰ Rooker has emphatically argued that the orthographical difference between דָּוִיד > דָּוִד is chronologically significant (1 Sam 24:9, 2 Sam 7:26 vs. 1 Chr 17:24, 2 Chr 5:1). He identifies the three letter דָּוִד as more archaic, in comparison to דָּוִיד. He observes, "In Ezra, Nehemiah and Chronicles, the name "David" occurs 271 times, all of which have the plene spelling." So, Rooker concludes that "one would expect the three-letter spelling to come from an author of the pre-exilic

---

Hebrew," *HS* 37 (1996): 21-37. Also, D. J. MaCarthy, "The Uses of *wᵉhinnçh* in Biblical Hebrew," *Biblica* 61 (1980): 330-342.

⁶⁷ Eskhult: Linguistic Development, 365. However, Longman had completely avoided the translation of הִנֵּה in his commentary on Song of Songs and Ecclesiastes. This is indeed a disturbing development as such attempts make the language of a book much more rigid and decorous than intended by the author himself. See, Tremper Longman III, *The Book of Ecclesiastes*, (Grand Rapids, MI: Eerdmans, 1998). Tremper Longman III, *Song of Song* (Grand Rapids, MI: Eerdmans, 2001).

⁶⁸ Total occurrences of הִנֵּה in BH is 1057 times. Its average occurrences in LBH – once in every three pages; EBH – once in every one and half pages. See, Ehrensvärd: Why Biblical Texts, 183.

⁶⁹ It has only one occurrence in Ezra (9:15), four occurrences in Nehemiah (5:5, 6:12, 9:36 [twice]) and three in Esther (6:5, 7:9, 8:7), while Qoheleth has six occurrences.

⁷⁰ See, David N. Freedman, "The Spelling of the Name 'David' in the Hebrew Bible," *HAR* 7 (1983): 89-102; Francis I. Andersen and A. Dean Forbes, *Spelling in the Hebrew Bible* (Biblica et Orientalia 41; Rome: Biblical Institute, 1986), 4-9.

period and a document containing the four letter plene spelling would have been composed in the post-exilic period."⁷¹ But Qoheleth uses the three-letter name in 1:1 and does not show preference to the later form.⁷² And also, The consistent orthography of לֹא, כֹּל throughout Qoheleth also points to the style of writing without plene spelling (except *belô'* in 10.11). It is thus within the parameters of the earlier development of Hebrew orthographic procedures. Seow thinks the orthography of Qoheleth is much more conservative than QH. However, it reflects the synthesis of orthographic elements, rather pointing to a linear development.

Ehrensvard argued that "when mentioning silver and gold together, there is a general tendency in EBH to mention silver first.. In LBH, the general tendency is to mention gold first."⁷³ Such observations were also made by Rooker.⁷⁴ Qoheleth uses the order as found in EBH. See, גַּם־כֶּסֶף וְזָהָב in 2:8 (see, 12:6 without *kesef*). This also is in conformity with the early use of the phrase כֶּסֶף וְזָהָב.

The presence of the relative particle שׁ which appears in very early passages such as Genesis 6:3, Jud 5:7 [twice], 6:17, 7:12, 8:26, 2 Kings 2:11, points to the possibility that it was not a distinctively late element.⁷⁵ In Qoheleth, שׁ occurs 67x along

---

⁷¹ Rooker: Diachronic Analysis, 138-139.

⁷² It should be noted that not only in Ezra, Nehemiah and Chronicles, but also in the Qumran Hebrew, the use of three letters for David was abandoned. All the extra-biblical documents points to the preference to the four letter name. *Ibid.*, 138-139.

⁷³ Ehrensvärd: Why Biblical Texts, 184.

⁷⁴ Rooker, *Biblical Hebrew in Transition*, 174-175.

⁷⁵ There are suggestions that שׁ belong to either northern origin or a vernacular element. However it also appeared in non-northern texts as Gen 6:3.

with אֲשֶׁר (89x).⁷⁶ The increasing use of שֶׁ in Qoheleth and in Song of Song (30x) is due to its poetical, conversational-type, swift presentation model and its chronological significance in Qoheleth remains undecided. ⁷⁷

The preference for direct speech in narrative is said to have been the hallmark of EBH in general. Frank Polak has attempted to establish such dichotomy between EBH prose and LBH prose.⁷⁸ Eskhult summarizes such position, "a swift narrative style, with many verbs, few nouns and short sentences, characteristic of, *inter alia*, the patriarchal narratives, is a token of oral tradition, and points to their (very) early origin. In contrast, an encumbered style, like that found in most late writings, is likely rooted in the scribal chancelleries, which suggest a late date."⁷⁹ Even, a general reading of Qoheleth is sufficient for anyone to recognize the conversational style of Qoheleth with participatory rhetorical questions, הִנֵּה, רְאֵה, etc points to a much more lively flavor in stylistics, rather than the "encumbered style" found in the LBH works.

---

⁷⁶ Isaksson observes that "in Qoheleth a kind of equilibrium is at hand: אֲשֶׁר 57%, שֶׁ against 43%... שֶׁ is used more often in chapters 1 and 2. From ch.3 on it is used more sparingly. אֲשֶׁר shows the highest frequency in ch. 7-9. Its frequency is relatively high also 1 Ch. 3-5." Isaksson, *Studies*, 149.

⁷⁷ Hurvitz: The Language of Qoheleth, 31-32.

⁷⁸ F. Polak, "The Oral and the Written: Syntax and Stylistics and the Development of Biblical Prose Narrative," *JANESCU 26* (1998): 59-105; F. Polak, "The Style of the Prologue in Biblical Prose Narrative," *JANESCU 28* (2001): 53-95; F. Polak, "Style is More Than the Person: Sociolinguistics, Literary Culture, and the Distinction between Written and Oral Narrative" in *Biblical Hebrew: Studies in Typology and Chronology*, ed. I. Young (JSOTSup 369; New York, 2003): 39-103.

⁷⁹ Eskhult: Linguistic Development, 356.

Late Features

Qoheleth has been identified as late work due to its linguistic features that are, according to the mainstream scholarship, characteristic of the LBH in general. Some of the lexicographical and grammatical features 'that are treated as late' are briefly discussed below.

Qoheleth's exclusive use of אֲנִי (28x) and his total avoidance of אָנֹכִי (0x) caused much speculation among scholars.[80] Generally, as Schoors observes, "אָנֹכִי is more frequent than אֲנִי in the older literature, whereas later on the frequency of the later increases."[81] And so, Schoors moves on to conclude that "all the evidence seems to point to a late phase of BH, close to MH, as far as Qoheleth's use of the 1cs personal pronoun is concerned."[82] However, this conclusion regarding the 1cs pronoun in Qoheleth has been recently disputed by Holmstedt.[83]

---

[80] Gordis, *Koheleth*, 364.

[81] Schoors: The Pronouns in Qoheleth, 71. He also gives the statistical data concerning the distribution of אֲנִי in the biblical books: אֲנִי occurs once in Gen 23:4; Jeremiah has אֲנִי 54 times and אָנֹכִי 37 times; Ezekiel has אֲנִי 138 times and אָנֹכִי only once (Eze 36:28). Similarly Malachi, Daniel, Nehemiah, and Chronicles have only one אָנֹכִי; Lamentations, Haggai, Ezra and Esther have אֲנִי to the exclusion of אָנֹכִי. Also in Qumran אֲנִי greatly outnumbers אָנֹכִי, and in MH, אָנֹכִי has practically disappeared being used only in biblical quotations. *Ibid.*, 71-72. It should be noted that the poetical books, except Job (14x), use אָנֹכִי sparingly: Psalms (13x), Proverbs (2x), Song (0x). אֲנִי is used in Job (27x), Psalms (40x), Prov (7x), Song (10x) and Qoh (28x). It should be noted that the mere appearance of a feature doesn't decide anything. Here, Qoheleth's self-reflective nature of arguments and observations plausibly warrant such high frequency of אֲנִי in contrast to other books.

[82] *Ibid.*, 72.

[83] See, Robert D. Holmstedt, "אֲנִי וְלִבִּי: The Syntactic Encoding of the Collaborative Nature of Qoheleth's Experiment," *JHS* 9/19 (2009): 2-27. In the conclusion of study, he writes: "Does Qoheleth really exhibit a "peculiar use of the pronouns," as Schoors asserts? Not at all. Qoheleth's

The phrase in 8:3, "כָּל־אֲשֶׁר יַחְפֹּץ יַעֲשֶׂה" has been used by Hurvitz to argue for a later period. Hurvitz cites five references (Ps 115:3, 135:6, Jonah 1:14, Isa 46:10 and Eccl 8:3) and observes that it was used only in conjunction with God or an earthly king and argues that it belongs to "the domain of jurisprudence."[84] According to him, the expression "he does whatever is good in his sight" is the standard idiom before 500 BCE, whereas "he does everything he desires" is the expression of choice after 500 BCE.[85]

Along with these features, host of other linguistic features are attributed to LBH influence on the language of Qoheleth: predominant use of participles, increasing use of שׁ with wide-range of grammatical application, the presence of the two Persian words, Aramaic influence, infrequent use of consecutive imperfects, the wide use of direct object marker, the feminine demonstrative *zôh*, the third masculine plural pronominal suffix for feminine plural antecedents, the negation of infinitive with אֵין, etc.

Observations and Evaluation

The first thing to observe about Qoheleth's language is that it does not represent a standard linear development of Hebrew

---

use of pronouns reflects syntactic options that are well represented throughout the biblical corpus of ancient Hebrew... the post-verbal pronoun strategy reflects the author's rhetorical skill and linguistic ingenuity, it is masterful use of language, neither odd nor ungrammatical." *Ibid.*, 20.

[84] A. Hurvitz, "The History of a Legal Formula: *kâl 'âser hâpâs 'âsâh*" VT 32 (1982): 257-67.

[85] *Ibid.*, 267; Also, Seow: Dating of Qoheleth, 664. Hurvitz believes that the comparative study of this Hebrew phrase with Aramaic helped him to pinpoint its lateness to Persian period. However, its predominant appearance with God might imply a religious language borrowed into court procedures later.

language. It shows the sporadic blend of 'early' and 'late' linguistic features throughout, be it orthographical, morphological, syntactical or lexical. Seow observes such linguistic amalgamation as follows, "the Hebrew of Qohelet cannot be identified with what we find in the Hebrew of Ben Sira, Qumran, Wadi Murabba'at, Nahal Hever and the Bar Kochba letters."[86] It cannot be aligned fully with the Hebrew of earlier books from the Pentateuch and former prophets because there are perceptible concentrations of 'late' features. At the same time, it also cannot be simply shelved with the later books as it does show more conservative use of linguistic features in comparison to the other later book. Thus, Seow's observation that "there are in fact more discontinuities between the language of Qohelet and Mishnaic Hebrew than there are continuities" is certainly valid.[87] It does leave us with the question of the cause behind such an unique formation of linguistic features. This issue will be discussed in the following section.

Approaching the Problem of Qoheleth's Language

The linguistically intricate nature of Qoheleth's language has to be approached by considering other important indicators which also contributes to the understanding of its language from a wider perspective. The naive circular reasoning, that the language of Qoheleth has a variety of linguistic features that corresponds to LBH and so it belongs to the later period, needs a thorough re-evaluation. This is necessitated in the light of the insufficiency of chronological models and the complexity of identifying the language of Qoheleth with that of the other LBH prose works. For, the language of Qoheleth epitomizes divergence in genre, stylistics and unconventional presentation

---

[86] Seow: The Dating of Qoheleth, 664.
[87] *Ibid.*, 665.

in contrast to the standard writings of any Biblical period. This section briefly discusses the influence of three important elements which the scholars of various periods perceived but not systematically applied, particularly in connection with Qoheleth and its language.

Influence of Genre upon Qoheleth's Language
In contrast to all of the LBH books which are mainly prosaic narratives, Qoheleth represents a kind of literature that can be categorized as "primarily a philosophical work rather than a book of religion. It seeks a rational understanding of human existence and a basis for ethics, through the application of human reason to observable data."[88] This fact, which was overlooked in the earlier researches on Qoheleth, was well expressed in the words of Gordis, "At the very outset, it must be borne in mind that Koheleth was a linguistic pioneer. He was struggling to use Hebrew for quasi-philosophic purposes, a use to which the language had not previously been applied."[89] This variation in literature type or genre has its serious bearing upon the language of the book as well. This will be shown from few examples below.

---

[88] R. B. Y. Scott, *Proverbs and Ecclesiastes*, AB (New York: Double Day, 1965), 196. Also, quoted by Fredericks, *Qoheleth's Language*, 28. Delitzsch also makes such observations: "it is, so to speak, a *philosophical treatise* in which 'I saw,' and the like, as the expression of the result of experience; 'I said,' as the expression of reflection on what was observed; 'I perceived,' as the expression of knowledge obtained as a conclusion from the process of reasoning." Delitzsch, *Ecclesiastes*, 199.

[89] Gordis, *Koheleth: The Man and His World*, 88. Also he develops this argument further in his 1955 article: "he [Qoheleth] is a pioneer in the attempt to use Hebrew for quasi-philosophic purposes, to express such ideas as "past," "present," "future," "recurrence," "moderation," etc." Robert Gordis, "Was Koheleth a Phoenician?" JBL 74/1 (1955): 104. However, the view that Qoheleth is the first of this kind is more of a general assumption based on the absence of such speculative rational works from the earlier period.

The overlooking of the genre of Qoheleth misled Dahood to conclude that Qoheleth's preference of generic use of אָדָם over אִישׁ is due to the Canaanite-Phoenician influence. This proposal was rightly rejected by Gordis, by noticing that due to its genre "Koheleth is speaking of "man" in the generic sense of "mankind."[90]

Again, the rare uses of *waw* consecutive imperfects (1:17, 4:1, 7) are argued to be the pointer to the later language of Qoheleth.[91] Similar infrequency of *waw* consecutives were also observable in The Manual of Discipline, which was attributed to its non-narrative character. This should be applied to Qoheleth as well. As Fredericks notes, "the reason for the sparse use in Qoh is equally obvious – Qoheleth is not representative of BH narrative either." Also Loretz makes this observation, "it is however to be considered, that the *waw* consecutive is not expected as often in a work like Qohelet as in narrative prose anyway."[92] This is another example of how genre influences the choice of grammatical constructions as well as lexical elements.

The frequent use of participles in Qoheleth (1:4-8; 2:14, 18, 19, 22; 3:9, 20, 21; 4:1, 5, 8, 17; 5:7, 19; 6:6, 10, 12; 7:26; 8:1, 7, 11-14, 16; 9:1, 5, 9, 16, 17; 10:3, 5, 19; 11:5; 12:5), which has been

---

[90] Gordis: Was Qoheleth a Phoenician?, 112. In Qoheleth, אָדָם occurs (49x)and אִישׁ occurs (7x) times; while the former refers to "mankind" in a generic sense, the later identifies "man" as individual.

[91] Seow explains this feature as vernacular element. See, Seow: The Dating of Qoheleth, 664.

[92] Loretz, quoted by Fredericks, *Qoheleth's Language*, 30. Even S. R. Driver, while studying Song of Songs, noted that the infrequency of *waw*-consecutive (Song 6:9,9) is due to the reason that "there is little occasion" for such feature to appear. S. R. Driver: A Treatise on the use of Tenses in Hebrew, 163. This conclusion can be legitimately applied to Qoheleth as well. Also, Crenshaw, *Ecclesiastes*, 50.

identified as a late feature,[93] is also clarified when this is seen from the genre point of view. Even though MH and Qoheleth use participles often, the contexts of the usages are very different. Qoheleth uses participles not just to denote present tense as in MH, but specifically he is using participles "because the book is largely concerned with statements of general truth."[94] Such usage of participles to convey gnomic concepts are well attested within BH and in wisdom literature. So, the simplistic equation of the frequency of the participles with LBH influence is unjustified and invalid.

Also, the unpredictable behavior of the definite article, which were explained due to Aramaic Translation theory as well as Phoenician influence, was negated with the simple explanation from the view of genre.[95] Gordis argued that "Many of the passages in Qoheleth are general statements, expressing some fundamental truth. In that event, Hebrew may use a noun in either the determinate or indeterminate state."[96] Such explanations of genre are also applied to nouns ending with *–ôn* and *–ût* which are frequent in Qoheleth. Fredericks argues that not only such nouns appear in all historical periods of Hebrew, but "these endings are indicative of abstract concepts, rather than concrete objects. Qoheleth is by its nature abstract, presenting universal truths, ethics and the deepest

---

[93] Generally, it is taken that imperfect was replaced by participles in Qoheleth, due to its late character. This was disputed by Isaksson, *Studies*, 123-125. Schoors, Pleasing Words I, 184-186. Also see, J. Joosten, "The Predicative Participle in Biblical Hebrew," *Zeitschrift für Althebraistik* 2 (1989): 128-159.

[94] Fredericks, *Qoheleth's Language*, 30.

[95] See, Zimmermann, F "The Aramaic Provenance of Qohelet," JQR 36 (1945/46), 21

[96] Gordis: The Original Language of Qoheleth, 82.

theological issues. It is expected then that this book would use abstract terminations more than would a historical book for example."[97]

These sample cases point to the fact that the language of Qoheleth should not only be approached from purely a chronological linguistic perspective. Any research into the language of Qoheleth should take into serious consideration the influence of genre upon its language. Simplistic comparisons of lexical-grammatical studies might lead to faulty conclusions if the inherent criteria of genre are overlooked.[98]

Colloquialism in Qoheleth's Language

The issue of colloquialism in Qoheleth has not received much attention until recently. The views of Schoors represent the mainstream scholarship in this regard. He states, "The presence of dialect in Qoh is a tricky question. As far as I can see, it can be neither disproved nor proved.... But again, the general distribution of a large number of [these colloquial] features taken together shows them to be late at the same time."[99] This observation betrays the limitation of his methodology which could not accommodate 'subjective' discussions like genre and dialectal influence into its scope.

This ignorance of colloquial aspect in the language of Qoheleth could also be one of the reasons for the theories proposed by Dahood. Young notes that "many of the examples

---

[97] Fredericks, *Qoheleth's Language*, 30-31.

[98] The observation of Fredericks is valid that "grammatical and lexical studies entail more than simplistic comparisons." Fredericks, *Qoheleth's Language*, 32. Also, Young, *Diversity*, 150-151.

[99] Schoors concede only one trait to colloquialism: "the relatively frequent lack of concord of subject and verb could be a trait of colloquial language." Schoors, *Pleasing Words I*, 223-224.

which led Dahood to his Phoenician theory for Qoheleth can be preferably explained as colloquialisms ..."[100] The constant indifference to such crucial factors in the language studies might cause the emergence of other unwarranted aberrant theories.

However, many of the linguistic divergences have been proposed to be attributed to Qoheleth's colloquial use. Fredericks argues that a linguistic study should consider these aspects of dialectal influence. He compares the 12 grammatical features of North Israelite dialect with Qoheleth's language and concludes that "the intriguing aspect of this list... is that Qoh has instances of nearly all the relevant traits to differing degrees."[101] Also, he presents a list of 13 cases of possible colloquialism from the earlier studies.[102]

It is not implausible as Barucq notes, "perhaps the author intentionally wrote his work in a related tongue of the spoken language with the object to draw attention and to make a lively style."[103] Seow also recognizes this aspect of colloquialism in Qoheleth:

"The Hebrew of Qohelet is like Mishnaic Hebrew only inasmuch as both languages are the literary deposits of

---

[100] Young, *Diversity*, 150. He gives two examples: the incongruence of number and gender, irregular use of definite article. *Ibid.*,150.

[101] Fredericks, *Qoheleth's Language*, 32-36.

[102] The list collected by Fredericks: 1) Anticipatory pronominal suffix (2:21, 4:12); 2) Discordant subject and predicate (1:10, 2:7); 3) Missing article; 4) Subject and predicate expressed in prepositional phrases (7:12); 5) Proverbial material; 6) First person delivery; 7) Few *waw*-consecutive construction; 8) Infinite absolute with *waw* (8:9, 9:11); 9) Third masculine plural noun (2:6,10; 10:9; 11:8; 12:1); 10) First singular pronoun; 11) Pronouns with את; 12) Feminine singular demonstrative; 13) The relative pronoun; 14) contractions (6:6, 4:3, 4:2). *Ibid.*, 36-46.

[103] Barucq, *Ecclesiastes*, 12.

popular, everyday speech... The language of the book, however, does not reflect the standard literary Hebrew of the postexilic period. Rather, it is the literary deposit of a vernacular... with its large number of Aramaisms and whatever jargons and dialectal elements one may find in the marketplace. The author was, after all, addressing the general populace—"the people"."[104]

Young also views the language of Qoheleth as "local literary dialect with much greater mixture of classical elements..."[105] This observation on the language of Qoheleth should be given some more careful treatment in the further investigations.

A Case for a Non-Literary Hebrew

This argument for non-literary Hebrew should be treated with much more care. Ferguson and Rendsburg,[106] and most recently Young have advocated this approach, with varied levels of differences. It holds tremendous implications to the whole spectrum of linguistic dating of biblical books. It maintains that linguistic varieties can be also explained synchronically. Young explains that in any given time in the history of Hebrew, there existed different kinds of languages employed for communication at home (informal and colloquial) and for official communication (formal and standard literary).[107] Along

---

[104] Seow: Linguistic Evidence, 664-666.

[105] Young, *Diversity*, 157.

[106] G. A. Rendsburg, *Diglossia in Ancient Hebrew* (AOS 72; New Haven, FT: Americal Oriental Soceity, 1990); "Linguistic variation and the foreign factor in the Hebrew Bible," *IOS 15* (1996): 177-190; "The Strata of Biblical Hebrew," *JNSL 17* (1991): 81-99; "Morphological evidence for regional dialets in ancient Hebrew," in *Linguistics and Biblical Hebrew*, ed. W. R. Bodine (Winona Lake, IN: Eisenbrauns, 1992): 65-88. Though Young has begun his research following Rensburg's trails, Rendsburg's commitment to Hurvitz's methodological principles has largely separated them to contrasting extremities. Young and Rezetko, *Linguistic Dating of Biblical Texts*, 30.

[107] Young, *Diversity*, 74.

with this, the presence of many nationals for trade purposes, co-existing immediate ethnic diversity in Jerusalem could have added to the linguistic variety of the Pre-exilic Judah.[108] This brings into question the foundations of the very theory that the language of the SBH books represents the language of the Pre-exilic period and the language of the LBH books are found in the post-exilic period.

If this non-literary Hebrew theory is granted, then there is a possibility to explain the linguistic diversities in Qoheleth using synchronic options, rather hard pressing them against the linear chronological models. Young observes, "Qoheleth is Aramaizing, Mishnaizing, and also seems to contain Persian loanwords. It does not fit in with the monolithic Standard Biblical corpus..." and this necessitates the need for a non-chronological model. He further explains that these linguistic varieties should be interpreted along with other evidences from the book, and only on the basis of its language, it cannot be categorized into a specific diachronic period.

Towards Formulating an Integrative Methodology
The current deadlock in the study of the language of Qoheleth has to be attributed to its methodological aspect. The incapability of the generally employed chronological model to categorize its language is due to Qoheleth's vast mixture of linguistic elements.[109] Both the chronological model and the

---

[108] Young argues "for the existence of diverse southern dialects in the biblical period." Young: Evidence of Diversity, 7-20. Also, Young, *Diversity*, 22-72. However, many scholars grant the diglossia situation for the post-exilic period doubt whether such situation really existed in the pre-exilic timese. See, Young and Rezetko, *Linguistic Dating of Biblical Texts*, 173-179.

[109] Holmstedt explains, "The linguistic profile of the book [of Qoheleth] is indeed unique and appears to be a mix of styles, stages, registers and dialects." Holmstedt: אֲנִי וְלִבִּי, 2.

non-chronological model have their own limitations and need to be further explained.

The diachronic model is too focused on reaching 'objective results' and so restricted in its scope; for it treats the influence of genre, colloquialism, registers, dialectal presence with suspicion. It mainly focuses its attention within biblical corpus and looks out only for epigraphical attestation. Its rigorous commitment to gaining objective results is worthy of commendation on the one hand, but on the other hand, this methodology does not allow its proponents to recognize alternative explanations for any linguistic variety. It assumes that linguistic varieties are effected into a language due to linear chronological changes. Such issues that affect the language change as styles, regional variations, foreign influence, impact of genre upon the language are, more or less, treated with passive suspicion and skepticism, as they seem to destabilize their 'objectivity' zone. So, it has become an exclusivist methodology that shuts its doors to the plausible realities that existed and caused the linguistic divergence in biblical literature. Also, as its confidence upon using epigraphical information as controls to date biblical books is swiftly dissolving into irredeemable oblivion, this methodology appears to be much more fragile than it did a decade ago.

On the other hand, the non-chronological model seeks to explain all the linguistic variations as synchronic diversities. It does not accept that the chronological development of Hebrew language is possible to trace within the Biblical corpus, at least by implementing the current chronological model. It proposes that the epigraphic references do not strictly correspond to the Biblical Hebrew, rather represent independent sub-linguistic stratum of linguistic developments that it cannot be used to date the biblical books. It does accept the influence of genre, colloquialism, local dialects and styles. However, such total rejection of diachronic development should be deemed problematic.

While it can be reasonably held that the Hebrew language did evolve throughout history and the changes were reflected in the languages used in the composition of the books, the criterion to determine such language changes are to be laid out with much more caution. It is true that language drifts can be an objective indicator for pointing to a certain period of composition for a book. However, there could be exceptions that affect such conclusion as well. While the diachronic model may be effective with the prose books, its implementation in Qoheleth is problematic and irrelevant; for Qoheleth doesn't have a early point for contrast as well as its genre is completely different from other LBH books. The indifference towards genre, styles, regional dialectal influence, and colloquialism in the linguistic studies are to be pointed out. A methodology, that concerns both the diachronic linguistic development as well as synchronic factors, is to be constructed to provide more accurate dating. The mystery surrounding the language of Qoheleth would remain unresolved until such options are made available in the future.

SUMMARY OF THE CHAPTER

This chapter pointed out the three current positions and the stalemate. And it became clear that the *impasse* is due to the methodological incapability of the current studies. After reviewing the methodologies and their inadequacies, the two major models were identified in today's scholarship: Hurvitz-Polzin's chronological model as well as Young's non-chronological model. A critical investigation into the Hurvitz-Polzin paradigm revealed its weaknesses and its narrow scope that *ipso facto* excludes many factors that contribute to linguistic change. And, the importance of approaching the language of Qoheleth from the linguistic diversity perspective was introduced after the works of Fredericks and Young. Also a reckoning, that a methodology that encompasses the diachronic sentiments of the text as well as synchronic factors is necessary for more comprehensive understanding of Qoheleth's language. Briefly, current approaches are incapable of assigning a specific date for Qoheleth purely on the basis of its language.

Conclusion

Michael O. Wise made the observation that, "even extremely conservative authors such as R. Ê. Harrison are forced by *the linguistic data* to acknowledge a postexilic date [for the book of Qoheleth]."[1] From the time of Delitzsch, the linguistic support for the dating of Qoheleth into post-exilic period, either Persian or later in to Hellenistic period (Ptolemaic), has become a scholarly fashion, even by the evangelical scholars.[2] It was believed that the linguistic criterion has overwhelmingly pointed to a late date. However, in the recent scholarship, not only the conclusions of the consensus, but also the methodologies that were employed to reach such conclusions were questioned.

---

[1] Michael O. Wise, "A Calque from Aramaic in Qoheleth 6:12; 7:12 and 8:13," *JBL* 109/2 (1990): 249-257. See, R. K. Harrison, *Introduction to the Old Testament* (Grand Rapids: Eerdmans, 1969), 1072-1078. Young also makes the similar observation, "I wonder whether the possibility of a pre-exilic reading of Qoheleth has not been entertained because the language evidence was so strong [for the post-exilic date]. See, Zevit: *Symposium*, 373.

[2] The latest commentary on Ecclesiastes by Bartholomew also takes the standard view that it originated in the Hellenistic period.

SUMMARY OF THE RESEARCH

While the introduction outlined the significance and purpose of engaging in the ensuing research, the first chapter traced the origin and development of the linguistic argument from Hugo Grotius (1644), the first scholar to notice the divergence in the language of Qoheleth. The important contributions of Delitzsch and its influential repercussions in the subsequent landscape of scholarship that are carried well into the 21st century by the repeated quoting of his legendary quotation on the language of Qoheleth followed. The age of theories that came out of the recognition, that the language of Qoheleth is late, was briefly discussed in the ensuing section. A major consensus was reached after Gordis, who stood in the tradition of Delitzsch and affirmed later date for Qoheleth's language. However, this *communis opinio* was breached by the recent studies by Isaksson, Fredericks, Young. Schoors has taken up the challenge and restated the position of mainstream scholarship in his massive two volumes. Though he conceded at various points, he defended the overarching conclusion that the language of Qoheleth represents a later stage in the diachronic development of the Hebrew language.

The following chapter (chapter 2) reviewed the major works of Isaksson, Fredericks, Schoors, Young and Seow, summarized their research and offered criticisms of their conclusions. While Isaksson has studied the structure of the verb as it stands in Qoheleth by employing the strategies of structuralism, he did contrasted it with the diachronic development in his conclusions that the verbal structure of Qoheleth is still distant from MH. Fredericks and Schoors pursued their investigation based on the lexico-grammatical methodology. While Fredericks allows the possibility of the influence of genre, colloquialism, dialectal influences, Schoors has stayed mainly within the lexical-grammatical paradigm in his study. Both of them reach varied conclusions by the analysis of their data.

CONCLUSION

While Fredericks proposes that Qoheleth was a pre-exilic composition, Schoors implies the later composition of Qoheleth into Hellenistic times. Young has argued that Qoheleth's language should be taken as "synchronic variety" of a particular time that elements of genre and colloquialism should be included in the study of the language. He prefers a late monarchic period dating for the book. Seow, on the other hand, supposes that the economic terminologies in Qoheleth sits well within the socio-economic context of the Persian world and adduces number of Persian period epigraphic materials to consolidate his position. The enigma of the language of Qoheleth remained unresolved.

With the brief summary of three major scholarly positions: early (Isaksson, Fredericks, Young), Middle/Persian period (Seow), and Late (Schoors), the third chapter begins addressing the issues related to the monotony of adduced arguments. It recognizes the repetitive results that the current studies tend to produce are due to the inadequacy of the implemented methodologies. The significant usage of the Hurvitz-Polzin paradigm was critically analyzed and its exclusivist tendencies were found to be incompatible with the wide range of factors that affect language change in a socio-historic setting. It has been noted that this chronological model was employed mainly for prose-narrative works and studies were conducted using the techniques of linguistic contrast between the assumed early-late literatures. Qoheleth's language, being very different from a prose narrative work and without any early point of reference, presents challenge to the chronological model and reveals its bankruptcy to date Qoheleth to a certain historical period. On the other hand, the non-chronological model, reading Qoheleth with its inherent monarchic background, recognizes the presence of colloquialism, influence of genre and assigns a date in the late monarchy. This approach indirectly allows the possibility of Solomonic provenance, with scribal touches that added a late coloring to the language of Qoheleth. However,

non-chronological model would need time to really shape up into a full-fledged field of study. The need for the integration of these methodologies was emphasized in the concluding section to understand Qoheleth, whose language represents greater divergence due to its unique philosophical-sapiential character.

IMPLICATIONS FOR FURTHER RESEARCH

Only based on the language, the book of Qoheleth cannot be dated late.[3] Having a conservative verbal structure, which is distant from MH, Qoheleth still falls mainly within the grammatical paradigm of BH. And Eaton's observation might hold true, "The language of Ecclesiastes does not at present an adequate resource for dating... [it] is probably of interest more in dialectology than chronology."[4] He holds that '[the language of] Qoheleth does not fit into any known section of the history of the Hebrew language.'[5]

The explanations of genre and colloquialism have given some horizons for further exploration. As our knowledge of the various factors that influenced and effected language drift and causes higher density of varied linguistic elements in a single literature grows, it holds much promise to understand the language of Qoheleth in clearer light and in the process also find the historical age of Qoheleth. As Schniedewind points out, "a greater attention to socio-linguistics and socio-political

---

[3] Young states that, "I'll be happy in ten years if someone has systematically destroyed my reading of Qoheleth, but not on the language basis. I don't think that can be done." He argues that linguistic evidence alone cannot warrant a date for a complex work like Qoheleth and it should be taken together with other evidences. Zevit: Discussion Session, 373.

[4] M. A. Eaton, Ecclesiastes (Downers Grove: Inter-Varsity Press, 1983), 17-19.

[5] *Ibid.*

history of the region should help contextualize future discussions of language change."[6]

The absence of specific historical indicators within the text poses serious problems for understanding the historical placement of Qoheleth. In spite of this huge obstacle, the scholarship of Qoheleth should be able to pay serious attention to the criteria of genre, colloquialism, etc to understand the uniqueness of the language of Qoheleth. The case for the non-literary Hebrew should be given some importance, as it might be intentional in composition of Qoheleth.

A comparative study of the verbal system of Qoheleth with that of Ben Sira should be undertaken to further investigate the language of Qoheleth.[7] Such study would illuminate our understanding of the Hebrew verbal system in the biblical as well as post-biblical era. It would also assist the decision making process of dating Qoheleth with much more precision from the linguistic vantage point.

The biggest challenge for the future studies is synthesizing the parameters of the chronological model with the non-chronological model. While chronological model assures of objective results, the non-chronological model takes wider factors into consideration. Both have to be interwoven into forming a more complete methodology to analyze a book like Qoheleth. But the challenge would be as how one defines the features belong to genre influence, dialectal influence, scribal additions, etc. However, the research horizons concerning the language of Qoheleth have not been exhausted.

---

[6] Schniedewind: Linguistic dating, 383.

[7] Isaksson had also done a study on the verbal system of Qoheleth (1987). Van Peursen has recently done a study on the verbal system of Ben Sira. But a comparative study between these two sapiential books is still due. See, W. Th. vanPeursen, *The Verbal System in the Hebrew Text of Ben Sira* (Leiden: Koninklijke, 2004).

Bibliography

PRIMARY SOURCES

Elliger, Karl and Willhelm Rudolph (eds). *Biblia Hebraica Stuttgartensia.* Stuttgart, Germany: Deutsche Bibelgesellschaft, 1997.

Fredericks, Daniel C. *Qoheleth's Language: Re-evaluating Its Nature and Date.* Ancient Near Eastern Texts and Studies 3. Lewiston, N.Y.: Edwin Mellen, 1988.

Isaksson, Bo. *Studies in the Language of Qoheleth: With Special Emphasis on the Verbal System.* Th.D diss., at Uppsala University, 1987.

Schoors, Antoon. *The Preacher Sought to Find Pleasing Words: A Study of the Language of Qoheleth – Part I.* Leuven: Uitgeverij Peeters, 1992.

_____, *The Preacher Sought to Find Pleasing Words: A Study of The Language of Qoheleth, Vocabulary – Part II.* Leuven: Uitgeverij Peeters, 2004.

Seow, C. L. *Ecclesiastes.* Anchor Bible. New York: Double Day, 1997.

_____, "Linguistic Evidence and the Dating of Qoheleth", *JBL* 115/4 (Winter, 1996) 643-666.

Shenker A., Y. A. P. Goldman, A. Van Der Kooij, and G. J. Norton (eds). *Biblia Hebraica Quinta, Fascicle 18: General Introduction and Megilloth.* Stuttgart, Germany: Deutsche Bibelgesellschaft, 2007.

Young, Ian. *Diversity in Pre-exilic Hebrew.* Tubingen: Coronot Books Inc, 1993.

SECONDARY SOURCES

Commentaries and Monographs

Andersen, Francis I. and A. Dean Forbes, *Spelling in the Hebrew Bible.* Biblica et Orientalia 41; Rome: Biblical Institute, 1986.

Bartholomew, Craig G. *Reading Ecclesiastes: Old Testament Exegesis and Hermeneutical Theory*. Roma: Editrice Pontificio Istituto Biblico, 1998.

_____, *Ecclesiastes*. BCOT. Grand Rapids, MI: Baker Academic, 2009.

Barton, G. A. *The Book of Ecclesiastes*. ICC. Edinburgh: T&T. Clark, 1908.

Berlejung, A., and P. van Hecke, eds. *The Language of Qohelet in Its Context: Essays in Honour of Prof. A. Schoors on the Occasion of His Seventieth Birthday*. Orientalia Lovaniensia analecta 164. Leuven: Peeters, 2007.

Bickerman, E. J. *Four Strange Books of the Bible: Jonah, Daniel, Koheleth, Esther*. New York: Schocken Books, 1967.

Burkes, Shannon. *Death in Qoheleth and Egyptian Biographies of the Late Period*. Atlanta, GA: Society of Biblical Literature, 1999.

Christianson, E. S. *Ecclesiastes Through the Centuries*. Blackwell Bible Commentaries. Malden, MA/Oxford: Blackwell Publishers, 2007.

Crenshaw, James L. *Ecclesiastes: A Commentary*. Philadelphia: The Westminster Press, 1987.

Delitzsch, F. *Proverbs, Ecclesiastes, Song of Solomon*, trans., M. G. Easton. Grand Rapids: Eerdmans, 1975.

Eaton, M. A. *Ecclesiastes*. Tyndale Old Testament Commentaries. Downers Grove: Inter-Varsity Press, 1983.

Fox, Michael V. *Ecclesiastes*. The JPS Bible Commentary. Philadelphia: The Jewish Publication Society, 2004.

_____, *Qoheleth and His Contradictions*. Decatur: The Almond Press, 1989.

Fredericks, D. C. *Coping with Transience*: Ecclesiastes on the Brevity of Life. Biblical Seminar 18. Sheffield, JSOT press, 1993.

Givon, Talmy. *Verb complements and Relative Clauses: A Diachronic case study in Biblical Hebrew*. Malibu, CA:1974.

Gordis, Robert. *Koheleth, The Man and His Wisdom: A Study on Ecclesiastes*. New York: Schocken Books, 1968.

Gordon, Amnon. *The development of the participle in Biblical, Mishnaic and Modern Hebrew*. Malibu, CA: 1982.

Hoffman, Joel. *In the Beginning: A Short History of the Hebrew Language*. New York: NYU Press, 2006.

Horowitz, Edward. *How the Hebrew Language Grew*. New York: Ktav Pub Inc, 1993.

Hurvitz, Avi. *A Linguistic Study of the Relationship of the Priestly source and the Book of Ezekiel, Cahiers de la Revue Biblique*. Paris: Gabalda, 1982.

Knobel, P. S. "Targum Qoheleth: A Linguistic and Exegetical Inquiry," Ph.D. diss., Yale University, 1976.

Levine, E. *The Aramaic Version of Qohelet*. New York: Genesis, 1978.

Loader, J.A. *Ecclesiastes: Text and Interpretation*. Michigan: William B. Eerdmans Publishing Company, 1986.

Lohfink, N. *Qohelet*. A Continental Commentary. Translated by Sean E. McEvenue. Continental Commentaries. Minneapolis: Fortress Press, 2003.

Longman, Tremper. *Song of Song*. Grand Rapids, MI: Eerdmans, 2001.

_____, *The Book of Ecclesiastes*. Grand Rapids, MI: Eerdmans, 1998.

Mavis, R. S. *The Epilogue of Ecclesiastes and the Meaning of the Book*. Ph.D. diss., Westminster Theological Seminary, 1999.

Murphy, R. E. *Ecclesiastes*. WBC 23A. Dallas: Word Publishers, 1992.

Ogden, Graham. *Qoheleth*. Sheffield: JSOT Press, 1987.

Perdue, Leo G. *The Sword and The Stylus: An Introduction to Wisdom in the Age of Empires*. Grand Rapids: Eerdmans, 2008.

Peter J. Leithart, *Solomon among the Post-Moderns*. Grand Rapids, MI: Brazos Press, 2008.

Polzin, R. *Late Biblical Hebrew: Toward an Historical Typology of Biblical Hebrew Prose*. Missoula, Mont.: Scholars, 1976.

Rendsburg, G. A. *Diglossia in Ancient Hebrew*. AOS 72; New Haven, FT: Americal Oriental Soceity, 1990.

Saenz-Badillos, Angel. *A History of the Hebrew Language*. New York: Cambridge University Press, 1996.

Saussure, Ferdinard de. R. Harris (trans. by), *Course in General Linguistics*. Paris: Open Court Publishing Company, 2006.

Schoors, Antoon (ed). *Qohelet in the Context of Wisdom*. Leuven: University Press, 1998

Segal M. A. *A Grammar of Mishnaic Hebrew*. Oxford: Clarendon Press, 1927.

Tyler, L. R. *The Language of Ecclesiastes as a Criterion for Dating*. Ph.D. diss., University of Texas, 1988.

Wallace, Daniel B. *Greek Grammar Beyond the Basics: An Exegetical Syntax of the New Testament*. Grand Rapids: Zondervan, 1996.

Waltke, Bruce K, and Michael O'Connor. An Introduction to Biblical Hebrew Syntax. Wionna Lake, IN: Eisenbrauns, 1990.

Whitley, Charles Francis. *Koheleth: His Language and Thought*. New York: de Gruyter, 1979.

Young, Ian and Robert Rezetko, *Linguistic Dating of Biblical Texts, Vol. 1and 2*. London: Equinox, 2008.

Zlotowitz, M. *Ecclesiastes: A New Translation with a commentary Anthologized from Talmudic, Midrashic and Rabbinic Sources*. Artscroll Tanakh Series. New York: Mesorah Publications, 1988.

Zuck, Roy B(ed). *Reflecting with Solomon*. Eugene, OR: Wipf and Stock Publishers, 1994.

Journal Articles

Adams, Jr., William James, L. La Mar Adams, "Language Drift and The Dating of Biblical Passages." *HS* 18 (1977): 160-164.

Alinei, Mario. "The Problem of Dating in Linguistics." *Quaderni di Semantica* 25/2 (2004): 211 – 232.

Archer, G. L. "The Linguistic Evidence for the Date of Ecclesiastes." *JETS* 7/3 (1969): 167 – 181.

Arnold, Bill T. and David b. Weisberg, "A Centennial Review of Friedrich Delitzschs "Babel Und Bibel Lectures." *JBL*121/3 (2002): 441- 457.

Bartholomew, Craig. "Qoheleth in the Canon? Current Trends in the Interpretation of Ecclesiastes." *Themelios* 24/3 (May 1999): 4 – 20.

Barr, James. "Determination and the Definite Article in Biblical Hebrew." *JSS 34* (1989): 307 – 335.

Berger, B. L. "Qohelet and the Exigencies of the Absurd." *Bib Int* 9/2 (2001):141-179.

Bhulam, Alain, "The Difficulty of Thinking in Greek and Speaking in Hebrew (Qoheleth 3:18, 4:13-16, 5:8)." *JSOT* 90 (2000): 101-108.

Binachi, Franceso. "The Language of Qoheleth: A Bibliographical survey." *ZAW* 105 (1993): 210 – 223.

Bolozky, Shmuel and Ora Schwarzwald. "On the Derivation of Hebrew Forms with the +ût Suffix." *HS* 33 (1992): 51 – 69.

Carasik, Michael. "Exegetical Implications of the Masoretic Cantilation Marks in Ecclesiastes." *HS* 42 (2001): 145-65.

Clemens, D. M. "Review of Schoors." *JNES* 56/2 (1997): 150 – 154.
Crenshaw, J. L., "Qoheleth in Recent Research." *HAR* 7 (1983): 41-56.
Cross, F. M. "The Oldest Manuscripts from Qumran." *JBL* 74 (1955): 153-162.
Dahood, M. J. "Qoheleth and Northwest Semitic Philology." *Bib* 43 (1962): 349-65.
———, "Qoheleth and Recent Discoveries." *Bib* 39 (1958): 302-18.
———, "The Language of Qoheleth." *CBQ* 14 (1952): 227-32.
———, "Canaanite-Phoenician Influence in Qoheleth." *Bib* 33 (1952): 30-52, 191-221.
———, "The Phoenician Background of Qoheleth." *Bib* 47 (1966): 264-82.
Davila, J. R. "Qoheleth and Northern Hebrew." *MAARAV* 5-6 (1990): 69-87.
Driver, S. R. "On Some Alleged Affinities of the Elohist." *JP* 11 (1882): 203-217.
Ehrensvärd, Martin. "Why Biblical Texts Cannot Be Dated Linguistically." *HS* 47 (2006): 177 – 189.
Eskhult, Mats. "The Importance of Loanwords in Dating Biblical Hebrew Texts." in *Biblical Hebrew: Studies in Chronology and Typology* (New York: T&T Clark, 2003): 8-23.
F. C. Burkitt. "Is Ecclesiastes a Translation?" *JTS* 23 (1921-22): 22-26.
Fischer, S. "Qohelet and 'Heretic' Harpers' Songs." *JSOT* 98 (2002): 105 – 121.
Fox, Michael V. "Qohelet's Epistemology." *HUCA* 58 (1987): 137 – 155 .
———, "The Meaning of *Hebel* for Qoheleth." *JBL* 105 (1986): 409 – 427.
———, "A North Israelite Dialect in the Hebrew Bible? Questions of Methodology." *HS* 37 (1996): 7 – 20.
Freedman, David N. "The Spelling of the Name 'David' in the Hebrew Bible." *HAR* 7 (1983): 89-102.
Gammie, John G. "Stoicism and Anti-Stoicism in Qoheleth." *HAR* 9 (1985): 169- 187.
———, "Review of Isaksson." *HS* 30 (1989): 148 - 152.

Gault, Brian P. "A Reexamination of "Eternity" In Ecclesiastes 3:11." *Bibliotheca Sacra* 165 (2008): 39-57.

Gentry, P. J. "Hexaplaric Materials in Ecclesiastes and the Role of the Syro-Hexapla." *Aramaic Studies 1/1* (2003): 5-28.

_____, "The Relationship of Aquila and Theodotion to the Old Greek of Ecclesiastes in the Marginal Notes of the Syro-Hexapla." *AS* 2/1 (2004): 63-84.

Ginsberg, H. L. "Ecclesiastes." In *Encyclopedia Judaica*, Edited by G. Wigoder, et al., vol. 6 (1971): 350-355.

Gordis, Robert. "Qoheleth and Qumran – A Study of Style." *Bib 41* (1960): 395-410.

_____, "The Original Language of Qoheleth." *JQR 37* (1946-47): 67-84.

_____, "The Translation Theory of Qoheleth Re-examined." *JQR 40* (1949-50): 103-16.

_____, "Was Koheleth a Phoenician?" *JBL 74* (1955):103-14.

_____, "The Original Language of Qoheleth." *JQR 37* (1946): 67-84.

Gordon, C. H. "North Israelite Influence on Postexilic Hebrew." *IEJ* 5/2 (1955): 85-88.

Hill, A. E. "Dating Second Zachariah: A Linguistic Reexamination." *HAR 6* (1982): 105-134.

Hirshman, M. "Rabbinic views of Qohelet." *JQR 91/3-4* (2001): 477-478.

Holmstedt, Robert. "The Distribution of *'ăšer* and *šeC-* in Qoheleth." *SBL* (2006): 1 – 15.

_____, "The Story of Ancient Hebrew *'ăšer*." *ANES 43* (2006): 7 – 26.

_____, "The Etymologies of Hebrew *'ăšer* and *šeC*." *JNES* 66/3 (2007): 177 – 191.

_____, "אֲנִי וְלִבִּי: The Syntactic Encoding of the Collaborative Nature of Qoheleth's Experiment," *JHS 9/19* (2009): 2-27.

Hurvitz, Avi. "The History of a Legal Formula: *kâl 'aser hâpâs 'âsâh*. " *VT* 32 (1982): 257-67.

_____, "Evidence of Language in Dating the Priestly Code: A Linguistic Study in Technical Idioms and Terminology." *Revue Biblique 81 /1* (1974): 24-56.

_____, "Hebrew and Aramaic in the Biblical Period: The

Problem of Aramaisms in Linguistic Research of the Hebrew Bible." in *Biblical Hebrew*: 34-37.

_____, "Linguistic Criteria for Dating Problematic Biblical Texts." *HA 14* (1973): 74-79.

_____, "Review of Fredericks." *HS 31* (1990): 144 – 154.

_____, "The Chronological Significance of Aramaisms in Biblical Hebrew." 234 – 240.

_____, "The Historical Quest for "Ancient Israel" and the Linguistic Evidence of the Hebrew Bible: Some Methodological Observations." *VT 47/3* (1997): 301-315.

_____, "Can Biblical Texts be Dated Linguistically? Chronological Perspectives in the Historical Study of Biblical Hebrew." in *Congress Volume: Oslo 199* (VTSupp 80), ed. A. LeMaire and M. Saebo. Leiden: Brill.

_____, "The Recent Debate on the Late Biblical Hebrew: Solid Data, Experts Opinions and Inconclusive Arguments." *HS 47* (2006): 191 – 210.

_____, "The Language of Qoheleth and Its Historical Setting within Biblical Hebrew." in *The Language of Qoheleth in Context* (Leuven: Peeters, 2007): 23-34.

Isaksson, Bo. "Correspondence." *HS 31* (1990): 275 – 276.

Jarick, John, "The Hebrew Book of Changes: Reflection on *hakhol hebel* and *lakkol zemen* in Ecclesiastes." *JSOT 90* (2000), 79-99.

Jong, S. de. "Qohelet and the Ambitious Spirit of the Ptolemaic Period." *JSOT 61* (1994): 85-96.

Joosten, Jan. "The Distinction Between Classical and Late Biblical Hebrew As Reflected in Syntax." *HS 46* (2005): 327-339.

_____, "The Predicative Participle in Biblical Hebrew." *Zeitschrift für Althebraistik 2* (1989): 128-159.

_____, "The Syntax of Volitive Verbal Forms in Qoheleth in Historical Perspective." in *The Language of Qoheleth in context* (Leuven: Peeters, 2007): 47 - 61.

Lane, D. J. "'Lilies That Fester': The Peshitta Text of Qoheleth." *VT 29/4* (1979): 481-490.

Khan, Geoffrey. "Review of Diversity." *VT 47* (1997): 409 – 412.

MaCarthy, D. J. "The Uses of *wᵉhinnçh* in Biblical Hebrew." *Bib 61* (1980): 330 – 342.

Miller, Douglas. B. "Qoheleth's Symbolic Use of lbh." *JBL 117/3* (1998): 437 – 454.

_____, "What the Preacher Forgot: The Rhetoric of Ecclesiastes." *CBQ* 62/2 (2000): 215 – 235.

_____, "Review of Pleasing Words II." *Biblica* 88/2 (2007): 260 – 262.

Morag, S. "Qumran Hebrew: Some typological observations." *VT* 38 (1988).

Mroczek, Eva. "Aramaisms in Qohelet: Methodological Problems in Identification and Interpretation." *Issues in Hebrew Philology*, Unpublished paper, (2008).

Muilenburg, J. "A Qoheleth Scroll from Qumran." *BASOR 135* (1954): 20-28.

Murphy, Roland E. "Review of Isaksson." *CBQ 51* (1989): 332 – 333.

Polak, F. "Style is More Than the Person: Sociolinguistics, Literary Culture, and the Distinction between Written and Oral Narrative." in *Biblical Hebrew: Studies in Typology and Chronology*, ed. I. Young (JSOTSup 369; New York, 2003): 39-103.

_____, "The Oral and the Written: Syntax and Stylistics and the Development of Biblical Prose Narrative." *JANESCU 26* (1998): 59-105.

_____, "The Style of the Prologue in Biblical Prose Narrative." *JANESCU 28* (2001): 53-95.

Rata, Cristian G. "Observations on the Language of the Book of Job." *S&I* 2/1 (2008): 5-24.

Rendsburg, G. A. "Linguistic variation and the foreign factor in the Hebrew Bible." *IOS 15* (1996): 177-190.

_____, "Morphological evidence for regional dialects in ancient Hebrew." in *Linguistics and Biblical Hebrew*, ed. W. R. Bodine (Winona Lake, IN: Eisenbrauns, 1992): 65-88.

_____, "The Strata of Biblical Hebrew." *JNSL 17* (1991): 81-99.

_____, "Review of Young." *HS 36* (1995): 135 – 140.

Robert D. Holmstedt, "אֲנִי וְלִבִּי: The Syntactic Encoding of the Collaborative Nature of Qoheleth's Experiment." *JHS 9/19* (2009): 2-27.

Rogland, Max. "Review of Schoors II." *RBL* (2006): 1-5.

Rooker, Mark F. "Diachronic Analysis and the Features of Late Biblical Hebrew." *BBR 4* (1994): 135 – 144.

Rudman, D. "A Note on the Dating of Ecclesiastes." *CBQ 61* (1999): 47-52.

Schmitz, Philip C. "Review of Diversity, by Young." *CBQ 57* (1995): 380 – 381.

Schniedewind, William M. "Steps and Missteps in the Linguistic Dating of Biblical Hebrew." *HS 46* (2005): 377 – 384.

Schoors, Antoon. "Review of Fredericks." *JBL 108/4* (1989): 698 – 700.

―――――――, "The Pronouns in Qoheleth." *HS 30* (1989): 71-90.

―――――――, "The Use of Vowel Letters in Qoheleth." *UF 20* (1988): 277-286.

Seow, C. L. "Qoheleth's Eschatological Poem." *JBL* 118/2 (1999): 209-234.

Snaith, John G. "Review of Fredericks." *JTS 41* (1990): 1543 – 155.

Steiner, Richard C. "Does the Biblical Hebrew Conjugation 'w' Has Many Meanings, One Meaning or No Meaning at All?" *JBL* 119/2 (2000): 229-267.

Strange, John. "Theology and Politics in Architecture and Iconography." *SJOT 5/1* (1991): 23-44.

Surburg, Raymond F. "The Influence of the Two Delitzsches on Biblical and Near Eastern studies." *CTQ, 47/3* (1983): 225-240.

Torrey, C. C.. "The Question of the Original Language of Qoheleth." *JQR 39* (1948-49): 151-60.

Ullendorff, E. "Meaning of *Qhlt*." *VT* 12/2 (1962): 215-215.

Weinberg, J. P. "Authorship and Author in the Ancient near East and in the Hebrew Bible." *HS 44* (2003): 157-169.

Whybray, Norman. "Review of Fredericks." *The Expository Times 100* (1989-2000): 390.

―――――――, "Qoheleth, Preacher of Joy." *JSOT 23* (1982): 87-98.

White, Marsha. "Review of Young's Diversity." *JBL 116/4* (1997): 730 – 732.

Wise, M. O. "A Calque from Aramaic in Qoheleth 6:12, 7:12, and 8:13." *JBL 109* (1990): 249 – 257.

Young, Ian. "Biblical Texts Cannot be Dated Linguistically." *HS 46* (2005): 341 – 351.

―――――――, "Evidence of Diversity in Pre-exilic Judahite Hebrew." *HS 38* (1997): 7-20.

―――――――, "Late Biblical Hebrew and Hebrew Inscriptions." in *Biblical Hebrew*, 276-311.

──────, "The Style of the Gazer Calendar and Some "Archaic Biblical Hebrew Passages." *VT* 42/3 (1992): 362 – 375.

Zevit, Tamar. "The Particles הִנֵּה and וְהִנֵּה in Biblical Hebrew." *HS 37* (1996): 21-37.

Zevit, Zinoy. "Symposium Discussion Session: An Edited Transcription." *HS 46* (2005): 321 – 376.

──────, "What a Difference a Year Makes: Can Biblical Texts be Dated Linguistically?" *HS 47* (2006): 83 – 91.

Zimmermann, F. "The Aramaic Provenance of Qohelet." *JQR 36* (1945/46): 17-45.

──────, "The Question of Hebrew in Qohelet." *JQR 40* (1949-50): 79-102.

www.ingramcontent.com/pod-product-compliance
Lightning Source LLC
Chambersburg PA
CBHW022131080426
42734CB00006B/318